creative mending techniques

beyond darning

Hikaru Noguchi

Ideas and instructions
for applying visible mending
to accessories and other
beautiful items

QUICK
THORN

Contents

Part 1

Basics of darning 23

Please note:
* The size of the materials and moulds given is only a guide.
* The works in this book are for your own use and to enjoy. Commercial sales, online or otherwise are prohibited.

Introduction

These new darned brooches and charms are the finishing touch: the cherry on your cupcake. By making a brooch with your own treasured fabrics and a personal creative touch you are expressing your individuality.

This book covers the basic and applied techniques of darning that I have developed and evolved over the past 10 years and shows you how to make brooches using these techniques. Some designs are more elaborate than others, but there are also many unique designs that people will ask you, 'what is that?' It's not just for the delight of the wearer, it starts a conversation with the viewer as well.

Among the treasured materials that I use are handkerchiefs received as souvenirs in the past, or clothes once worn by loved ones, bringing evocative memories with them, such as the clothes your child wore when they were little. It's hard to put scissors into your memories and feel that you are destroying these precious fabrics, but then, not to do anything with them seems such a waste. Cutting a 10cm square of the treasured cloth is a great way to make a gentle start.

By dismantling clothes that could not be thrown away and by making brooches with materials that you have fond memories of, you'll feel closer to your memories, and you'll be able to create works that are uniquely yours. Of course, the material for the darning brooch can also be new or leftover cloth from your stash – ribbons that were saved, charms from a broken necklace, buttons and beads found at a flea market, etc. Just by sewing a few things together, your favourite items that were stuck on the shelf at home will begin to shine and have some meaning for you. If you find something you like among the works in this book, try using it as a reference, rather than reproducing the design exactly. Try imitating it 'your way' and sewing it 'your way'. Doing it your own way becomes an important part of what makes your work unique. Then they will be your treasures, not mine.

Your patches can be made into brooches and can also be sewn onto damaged parts of clothing or accessories as a darning patch. Add a string or chain to make a charm for your bag. Make a collage brooch using the scraps left over from sewing making use of the shapes created by chance to invent your own abstract painting. Thread the remaining fabric onto a kilt pin and you can create an intriguing pin brooch too.

If you are not good at sewing or have difficulty sewing, you can try using craft glue. There are no rules in this book that say, 'you have to do it this way'. Just add your imagination to your usual mending and needlework and get creative. If you're worried about the freedom of being told that you can make things however you like, try unravelling your own ideas about how things should be done. Try your hand at needlework with faith that 'your way' is the right way. We hope that your interest expands to make treasures small enough to fit in the palm of your hand.

Hikaru Noguchi

Tools for darning and brooch making

Introducing everything from essential tools for darning and making brooches, to useful things to have in your toolbox. Learn about the different types and choose the ones that suit you best.

Basic tools

You can start darning right away with a darning mushroom, thread, needle and scissors. Just use the tools you have on hand.

Hair tie
Used to secure cloth to the darning mushroom. You can use a hair elastic or a rubber band.

Embroidery hoop
A tool for holding cloth in place. Tautness makes it easier to darn and prevents twisting.

Darning mushroom *
A mushroom-shaped tool specifically designed for darning. You can also use a ladle or a tennis ball.

Cutting scissors
Save your best shears just for fabric and they will stay sharper for longer.

Ruler
Used to measure the amount of cloth or for drawing lines.

Thread scissors
Small, sharp scissors are great for cutting thread and detailed work.

Tailor's chalk
Used to mark cloth and easily brushed off afterwards.

Needles
Embroidery needle #5 extra fine, #3 medium-fine, #15 has a blunt tip, for use on knitwear.

Wire needle threader
A useful item for threading tricky materials.

Basting thread
Used for temporary tacking stitches to prevent cloth from shifting.

Pins
Fine dressmaking pins will leave no trace on your work.

Hook-type threader *
Easily hook multiple threads onto the hook and thread through the needle.

✳ An original Hikaru Noguchi product

Materials for brooches

Introducing the materials needed to make a brooch. You don't have to sew a brooch pin, just thread a kilt pin through it to create a wonderful brooch.

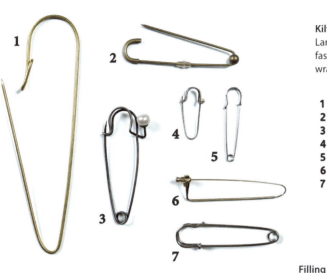

Kilt pins
Large safety pins useful for fastening shawls and traditional wraparound skirts.

1 Giant wire kilt pin
2 Threaded kilt pin
3 Silver and pearl kilt pin
4 Silver kilt pin
5 Kilt pin
6 Stainless steel pin
7 Pin purchased in an African market

Filling
Polyester or cotton toy stuffing for filling soft brooches. You can also use scraps of cloth or thread.

Knit or bulb pins
These bulbous spins have no coils so won't damage the fabric.

Locking brooch pin
A sew-on brooch pin that can be locked to prevent the brooch falling off.

Button badges

Macaron moulds
This is the base of the macaron brooch, use covered-button parts, badge-making kits, or the lids of jam jars. These come in many sizes and you can use them as darning mushrooms too.

Macaron mould
(plastic button)

Bottle lid

Useful tools

These are great shortcuts for those labour-intensive tasks, such as basting or finished edges and will speed up your work.

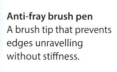

Glue for temporary fixing
Fix patches without sewing with this water-soluble glue that dries clear.

Anti-fray brush pen
A brush tip that prevents edges unravelling without stiffness.

Recommended types of thread and needles for darning

1 Sashiko thread
Cotton thread for sashiko, a traditional Japanese stitch. It has a rustic, matt texture.

Needle #3

2 Button thread
Highly-spun and durable, designed for attaching buttons. One strand is great for darning.

Needle #3 or #5

3 #8 embroidery thread
Floss #8 features an elegant, pearly lustre. The thickness is almost the same as sashiko thread.

Needle #3

4 #25 embroidery thread
Japanese thread with reduced shine. 100% cotton. Untwist and use one or two strands.

Needle #3 or #5 or #15

5 Linen thread *
A natural fibre thread made from flax. This refreshing yarn is used for summer sweaters.

Needle #3 or #5

6 Lamé thread
A thread studded with sparkling glitter. Use one that is smooth so easy to stitch.

Needle #3 or #5

✳ An original Hikaru Noguchi product

Although it is simply called thread, there are many different types that vary in colour, thickness, purpose, material and manufacturing method. To start just choose one in your favourite colour.

7 Merino wool *
From Merino sheep, this wool has fine fibres and is slightly elastic. Perfect for darning.
Needle #3

8 Thick wool yarn
This straight yarn is recommended for beginners. Some wool may shrink in the wash and become stronger.
Needle #3 or #5

9 Silk mohair thread
Light and fluffy, this is also space-dyed so it changes colour.
Needle #3

10 Fluorescent yarn
These vivid colours can only be acheived with 100% acrylic. Untwist and use one or two strands as needed.
Needle #3 or #5

11 Thin bouclé *
Bouclé means 'in a loop' and this mohair yarn is characterised by the small loops in the thread.
Needle #3

12 Chunky bouclé *
This bouclé has a shine or lustre, and creates a great fluffy surface.
Needle #15

Fabrics for darning brooches

Most of the bases and patches used for brooches are made from scraps or clothes before they are disposed of. If you are using new cloth, it's a good idea to wash and iron it before use.

1 Sheeting (cotton/linen blend)	**10** Wool (cut from a sweater)	
2 Linen fabric (cut from an apron)	**11** Corduroy	
3 Oxford cotton (cut from a shirt)	**12** Cotton jersey (an old T-shirt)	
4 Fleece (cut from a jacket)	**13** Printed cotton	**18** Machine knit (cut from a wornout sweater)
5 Velveteen	**14** Denim (from old jeans)	
6 Cotton chambray (from an old skirt)	**15** Crochet motif (part of an old cardigan)	**19** Felt
7 Cotton lawn (from a blouse)		**20** Polyester print (an old skirt)
8 Cotton voile	**16** Plain weave woollen fabric	**21** Wool ribbon
9 Cupra (from the lining of a skirt)	**17** Cotton tweed	**22** Velvet ribbon

Part 1

Basics of darning

Starting and finishing stitches

These are the basics of needlework, from preparation before stitching, to thread tidying afterwards. Using an embroidery hoop and cutting up clothes will expand your skills.

Threading a needle

This method makes a crease in the thread and pushes the fold through the eye of the needle to make it easier.

1 Place the side of the needle eye on the pad of your index finger about 3cm from the end of the thread.

2 Fold the thread in half over the needle and pull out the needle, while squeezing the thread.

3 Separate your finger tips and you can see a glimpse of the crease in the thread.

/ Don't move your fingers too far apart! \

 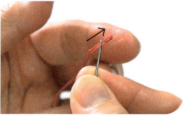

4 Pass the folded edge through the eye of the needle.

5 Pull through and then pull just one end of the thread.

How to use a threader

These make it easier: there are wire and hook types of threader, so choose one for the size of thread and needle.

Diamond wire type

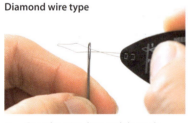 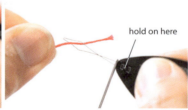 

hold on here

1 Pass the wire diamond through the needle hole.

2 Pass the thread through the wire diamond.

3 Hold on to the handle as you pull the thread through the eye.

Hook type

1 Insert the hook into the eye of the needle.

2 Pass the thread over the hook.

3 Pull the threader and the thread through the eye.

Starting knot

To prevent the stitched thread coming loose, make a knot at the end of your thread before sewing. This method prevents the ends from becoming tangled.

1 Thread the needle and place the tip of the needle where you want to make the knot.

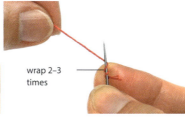

wrap 2–3 times

2 Wrap the thread around the needle 2–3 times.

3 Hold the thread firmly with your fingertips.

4 Pull the thread and bring the knot to the end of your length.

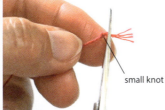

small knot

5 If the end of the thread is too long, cut it with scissors.

Finishing

There are basically three types of finishing after darning. When making a brooch, make sure to fasten the embroidery so that it does not unravel.

Cut leaving a tail

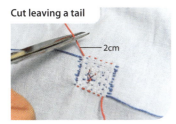

2cm

Cut the thread leaving about 2cm at the end. The end will almost never come out, even if you leave it.

Pass back through a seam

1.5–2cm

1 Pass the needle through the stitches on the wrong side.

2 Pull the thread through.

3 Trim the excess thread with scissors.

French knot

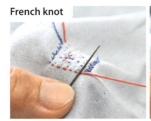

1 Place the needle over the end of the last stitch.

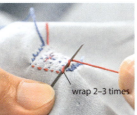

wrap 2–3 times

2 Wrap the thread around the needle 2 or 3 times.

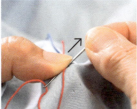

3 Hold the wound thread firmly while pulling the needle.

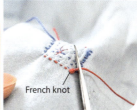

French knot

4 Trim the ends.

How to use a darning mushroom

Mushrooms are useful when darning. Most of the projects use mushrooms, but you can use any method you like, such as an embroidery hoop or stitch without anything at all if you prefer.

1 Apply the darning mushroom from below the damaged area, with right side up, and grip the handle. Spread the gathered fabric and hold.

2 While still holding the handle, place a hair tie around the base of the mushroom.

3 Wrap the hair tie 2–3 times to secure it in place. If your elastic doesn't have a loop, tie only once (don't tie it too tightly or it will not come undone).

4 The damaged part is at the centre of the dome of the darning mushroom and the fabric is neither too loose, nor too tight.

When darning the edges

Set the fabric so that the edge is about 2-thirds of the way over the darning mushroom and secure with a hair tie.

When the area to be mended is large

When darning a wide area or sewing a large patch, you can make the work easier by using can lids or books, or what's available, instead of a darning mushroom.

Using an embroidery hoop

If you use an embroidery hoop, you will have more access to the back of the work. If the fabric is too loose it will be hard to stitch, so keep the fabric as taut as possible. If it's stretchy fabric, be careful not stretch it too much!

1 Divide the hoop into an inner and outer frame and place the fabric over the smaller, inner frame.

2 Fit the outer frame so that the damaged area is in the centre.

3 Pull the surrounding cloth to prevent it from sagging and turn the screw to tighten.

Cut clothes into cloth

Sweater

If you like the material, but no longer wear it, why not cut it up and turn it into cloth? Even if you don't think you'll ever wear it again, it's heartbreaking to cut things up. Sometimes I say, 'Thank you' and cut the sleeves and hem first. After cutting it into larger pieces, washing and ironing, it returns from clothing to cloth. Look at the curve of a sleeve or the pocket of a shirt and you may find inspiration for your designs.

Jeans

By washing and ironing the fabric cut from clothes, you can use it to make darning patches or brooches.

Darning with running stitch

Lots of mending is based on running stitch, which is the most basic of hand-stitches. You can sew more efficiently by working several stitches at a time. It's suitable for reinforcing lightly damage areas, and for sewing patches or gathering.

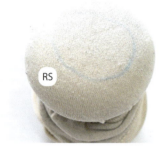

1 Position the cloth on the centre of your darning mushroom and mark the area to be mended with chalk.

2 Cut a 50cm length of yarn and thread the needle. Insert the needle about 3cm outside your mending area.

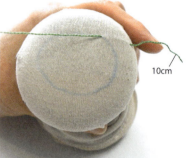

3 Pull the thread, leaving an end about 10cm long. You can finish the ends later.

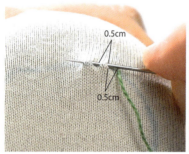

4 Insert and remove the needle at 0.5cm intervals. Sew 2 to 3 stitches.

5 Pull the thread through (without pulling the end through).

6 Repeat steps 4–5. It doesn't matter if the stitches are uneven.

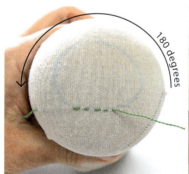

7 Once you have sewn all the way to the edge, rotate the mushroom 180 degrees.

8 Insert the needle 0.2–0.3cm above the first row and sew in the same way as steps 4 and 5.

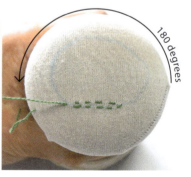

9 Once you have sewn all the way to the edge, rotate the mushroom 180 degrees again.

USES
For lightly damaged, eye-catching socks

MATERIALS
#8 embroidery thread, button or sewing thread.

10   After sewing several rows, gently pull the fabric to correct any kinks or wrinkles.

11   When the thread is short, bring the needle out about 3cm from the edge and leave the end.

12   Rotate the darning mushroom 90 degrees and with a new thread repeat step 2.

13   Repeat steps 4–5 with the new thread, working across the previous stitching.

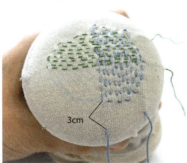

14   When you have worked halfway bring the needle out about 3cm from the edge.

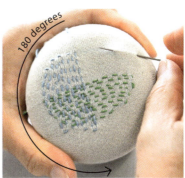

15   Rotate the mushroom 180 degrees and start a new thread in the same way as step 2.

16   Repeat steps 4–10 with the new thread.

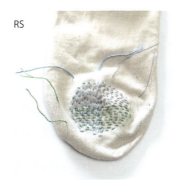

17   When you have finished, remove the mushroom.

18   Pull out the thread ends to the wrong side and finish (see P25).

Darning with seed stitch

These small stitches are so named because they look like sesame seeds. The back is heavily covered, making the fabric more durable and stretchier than regular stitching. You can also work it on the reverse if you like the look. Seed stitch is useful for adding a subtle accent of colour to your work.

1 Place your cloth on the mushroom and mark the area you want to repair with chalk.

2 Cut a 50cm length of yarn and thread the needle. Insert the needle about 3cm outside your mending area.

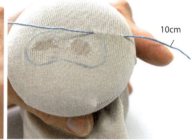

3 Pull the thread, leaving an end about 10cm long. You can finish the ends later.

4 Insert the needle 0.1cm back and take it out 0.5cm ahead.

5 Pull the thread. You have made one seed stitch.

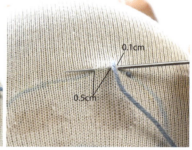

6 Insert the needle 0.1cm back, take it out 0.5cm ahead and pull the thread.

7 When you reach the edge of the mark, rotate the mushroom 180 degrees.

8 Insert the needle 0.2–0.3cm above the first row and repeat steps 4 and 5.

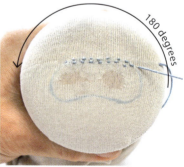

9 Once you reach the edge again, rotate the mushroom 180 degrees and repeat.

USES
Socks that
have become
worn out

MATERIALS
Button thread
or #8 embroidery
thread

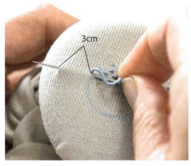

10 When the thread is short, bring the needle out about 3cm away from the edge and leave an end of about 10cm.

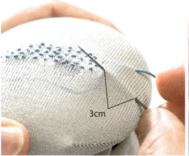

11 With a new length of yarn, thread the needle and insert it about 3cm outside your mending area.

12 Leave an end about 10cm long and repeat steps 4–5.

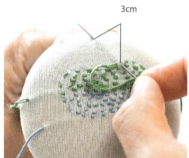

13 Work to the end and take the needle out about 3cm outside the marked area.

14 This is what the right side will look like when you have finished.

15 Remove the darning mushroom.

16 Pull the ends through to the wrong side. Turn the sock inside out and finish the ends (see p25).

**running stitch
+
seed stitch**

Shake it up by doing some mends with the wrong side facing. Darning your socks while they are only lightly damaged will make them last longer.

Working with strips of fabric

Cut or torn cloth is attached with running or seed stitches. Roughly sewn frills and torn fabric creates a decorative and three-dimensional finish.

Delicate frills

CLOTH	THREAD
Cotton lawn	Sashiko

1 Thread the needle and tie a knot in the end. Sew a big running stitch down the centre of a strip of cloth.

2 Make 10–15 running stitches in a long row (see P28).

3 Pull the thread and gather the fabric to create a ruched effect.

seed stitch (p30–31)

4 Place temporarily while you decide where to attach your new motif.

5 Stitch in place by straddling the existing thread and make a few stitches to secure.

6 Create another motif and attach in the same way.

Frayed strips

CLOTH	THREAD
Ticking	Sashiko

1 Make a slit at the edge of the fabric with scissors.

2 Tear by hand from where you made the cut.

3 Make a few more strips in the same way.

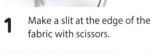

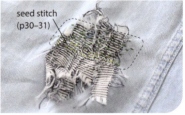

seed stitch (p30–31)

4 Apply temporary adhesive to the area to be mended.

5 Place the strips randomly.

6 Attach the patch with seed stitch in one area as shown.

Brooches made with running and seed stitch

RAISED SEED STITCH
The basic method is the same as seed stitch. When pulling the thread don't pull it all the way through, leaving a loop.

cloth

No. 01 Lunch plate

Finished size: 6cm

A seed stitch (P30–31)

same as **A**

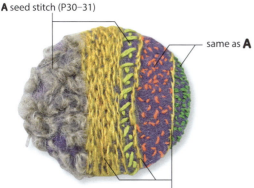

reverse seed stitch (P30–31)

How to make

1 Stitch as shown.
2 Finish into a macaron brooch (P63-65).
3 Attach the brooch pin (P60-61).

This example uses only seed stitch, which changes depending on the choice of thread.

MATERIALS
Front: cotton jersey 13 x 13cm (cut from a T-shirt)
Filling: soft toy stuffing
Back: Felt 9 x 9cm
Macaron mould 6cm diameter

No. 02 Cinnamon flower

Finished size: 10 x 10cm

raised seed stitch

seed stitch (P30–31)

chain stitch (P54)reverse

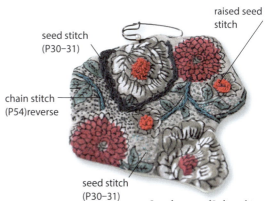

seed stitch (P30–31)

I used scraps of Indian chintz, cutting to fit in as many of the flower motifs as possible.

How to make

1 Stitch as shown above.
2 Finish into a soft brooch (P56-57).
3 Attach a kilt pin (P62).

MATERIALS
Front and back: Indian chintz (20 x 20cm)
Filling: soft toy stuffing

No. 03 After chaos

Finished size: 8cm x 26cm

How to make

1 Stitch as shown in the picture.
2 Finish into a soft brooch (P56-57).
3 Attach a kilt pin (P62).

wool felt   cotton canvas   linen   tapestry fabric

printed cotton

cotton lawn

MATERIALS
Front and back: cotton and linen fabrics (2 pieces 35 x 15cm)
Filling: soft toy stuffing

This brooch was born through trial and error, making use of the shape of the scraps. Since it is a complex shape, I finished it with simple stitches.

darning with appliqué (P50)
+
running stitch (P28–29)

Darning with blanket stitch

Blanket stitch is perfect for repairing the damage to edges. It is recommended for cuffs and the hems of sweater and sweatshirts, as it is able to stretch with your garment.

1 Set the fabric so that the edge is two thirds of the way over the darning mushroom, Cut a strand of 50cm and thread the needle. Insert the needle 0.5 to 1cm from the edge and bring it out on the wrong side.

2 Pull the thread, leaving an end of about 10cm without tying a knot.

3 Insert the needle to the left, about 0.3–0.5cm along the edge.

4 Move the thread to the left behind the needle.

5 Pull the thread lightly.

6 Insert the needle again and repeat steps 3 and 4.

USES
Mending damaged
cuffs on sweaters

MATERIALS
Cashmere
yarn

Part 1 Basics of darning | Darning with blanket stitch

7 Pull the thread lightly.

8 Repeat steps 3 to 5. You can make the stitches spaced out, the same lengths or irregular.

9 To finish, remove the darning mushroom, insert the needle from the back to the front as in steps 3 and 4, with the thread moving from left to right.

10 Pass the needle through the stitches on the wrong side. Then finish the end at the beginning of the row in the same way (see P25).

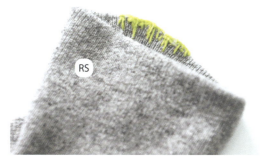

11 Trim any excess threads with scissors.

12 The blanket stitch is complete. Depending on the level of damage, we recommend layering seed stitch darning over the top for strength.

Darning with honeycomb stitch

This is a versatile method that can be used for stains and worn-out areas, as well as areas with holes. The stitches are elastic and won't rub your skin. The underside has a dotted pattern like fireworks, so you might want to work it in reverse.

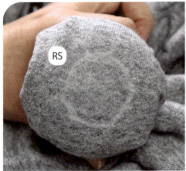

1 Place the garment on the darning mushroom and mark the area with chalk.

2 Cut a 50cm length of yarn and thread the needle. Insert the needle about 3cm outside your mending area.

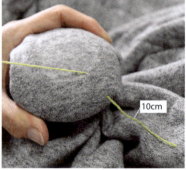

3 Pull the thread, leaving about 10cm of the thread, without using a knot.

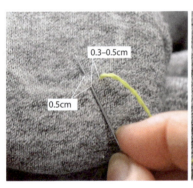

4 Insert the needle 0.3–0.5cm to the left, and come up about 0.5cm above.

5 Pull the thread around the needle, from right to left.

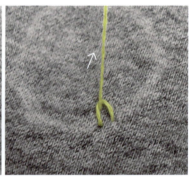

6 Pull the thread lightly. Be careful not to pull too tightly.

7 Insert the needle 0.3–0.5cm to the left, and come up about 0.5cm above. Pass the thread behind from right to left.

8 Repeat step 7 around the chalk mark. When you run out of thread, remove it from the needle and change for a new length.

9 Using the new thread, repeat step 4, leaving the ends.

USES
Covering stains
on sweatshirts
and for socks

MATERIALS
Wool, silk-mohair
and cashmere
threads

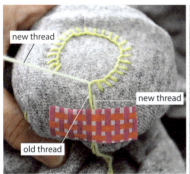

10 Leave about 10cm of the new thread and secure both old and new ends with some washi tape to keep them out of the way.

11 Repeat step 7 with the new thread. When you reach the first stitch, pass the needle under.

12 Pull the thread up and get ready for the next round.

13 Insert the needle from the inside the next loop. Bring the needle out 0.5cm above with the yarn behind.

14 Repeat step 13 until you reach the end of the next round and connect with the first stitch to complete.

15 Repeat steps 13 and 14 until the centre is filled. When the thread is too short, repeat steps 8 and 9.

16 Insert the needle into the centre, bringing it outside the darned area. Remove the mushroom.

17 Pull the ends to the wrong side and finish the threads in your chosen way (see p25). This could also be the right side if you like.

18 Your honeycomb stitch darning is complete.

Parallel honeycomb stitch

This is a method of darning by layering blanket stitches in horizontal lines. The front and back are both interesting, so you can wear it either way. You can also make triangles as well as rectangles.

1 Position the fabric on a mushroom and mark the area to sew with chalk. Cut the thread to be used to about 50cm.

2 Thread the needle and insert about 3cm away from the chalk mark, and bring the needle out at the bottom left of the area.

3 Pull the thread and pass it to the bottom right of the area. Leave an end of about 10cm with no knot.

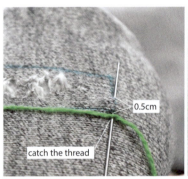

4 Insert the needle through the thread and into the fabric, coming out about 0.5cm above.

5 Wrap the thread from right to left around the needle.

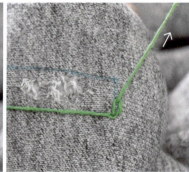

6 Pull the thread lightly.

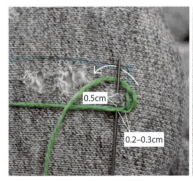

7 Catch the thread again 0.2cm–0.3cm to the left and come out 0.5cm above. Wrap the thread around the needle.

8 Pull the thread lightly to complete the stitch.

9 Repeat steps 7 and 8 until you reach the end of your marked area.

USES
Sweatshirt that
is frayed

MATERIALS
Wool yarn

Part 1 Basics of darning | Parallel honeycomb stitch

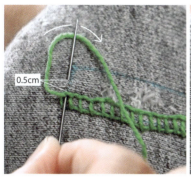

10 Insert the needle into the first row, and come out 0.5cm above, wrapping the thread around the needle from left to right.

11 Pull the thread lightly, then repeat steps 7–8 along the row.

12 When you get to a hole, carry on in the same way. When the thread gets too short, remove it from the needle.

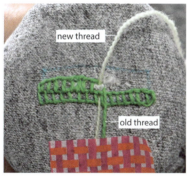

13 Thread the needle again and insert into the stitch, using the new thread to wrap the needle. Secure the ends with tape.

14 Repeat steps 7–8. You may want to skip a stitch, or put two stitches in the first stitch.

15 When the marked area is complete, finish the last stitch and bring the needle out about 3cm away.

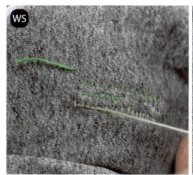

16 Trim the thread. Remove the darning mushroom and finish the threads (see p25).

17 Finish all the threads in the same way.

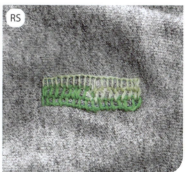

18 Darning with the parallel honeycomb stitch is complete.

Honeycomb flower stitch

This is a method of darning with flowers using blanket stitch. It can used as a design accent when mending small holes. Increasing the number of petals will create more volume and texture to your design.

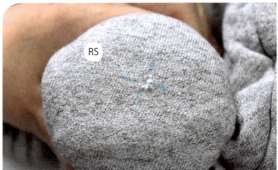

1 Position your fabric on the mushroom and mark the area to be darned with a cross in chalk. Cut a length of your chosen thread, about 50cm.

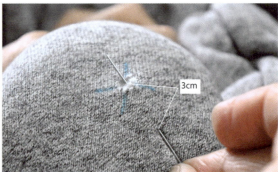

2 Insert the needle about 3cm away and bring it out in the centre of the mark.

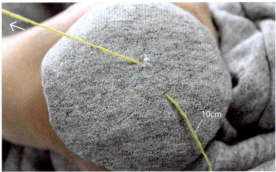

3 Pull the thread, leaving a 10cm tail.

4 Take the needle in at the edge of the mark, and pull it out at the centre.

5 Wrap the thread around the needle from right to left.

6 Pull the thread.

7 Insert the needle about 0.3–0.5cm to the left and bring it out at the centre again, wrapping the thread from right to left.

8 Repeat step 7 until you have gone all the way around, then pick up the thread of the first stitch.

9 Pull the thread. If the hole is not covered, repeat steps 4 to 6.

10 Insert the needle into the centre.

11 Finish the threads. Remove the darning mushroom, bring the needle to the back and pass the needle under the threads at the back (see p25).

12 The honeycomb flower is complete.

Tambourine stitch

USES
Sweaters with
small holes

MATERIALS
Wool yarn

This is worked from the centre outwards, allowing you to expand the circle. It's useful for covering small stains and can be versatile, made into a fan or used back to front.

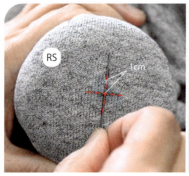

1 Mark the area to be mended with a chalk cross. Insert the needle in the centre and come out 1cm above.

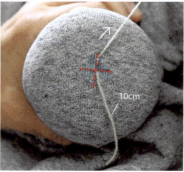

2 Pull the thread. Leave a tail of about 10cm without tying it in a knot.

3 Insert the needle in the centre and bring out 0.3–0.5cm away. Wrap the thread from right to left behind the needle.

4 Pull the thread gently. It should look like a petal, or half a heart.

5 Insert the needle into the centre and bring it out to the left. Pass the thread behind from right to left and pull the needle.

6 Repeat step 5 until you complete the circle, then pick up the thread of the first stitch.

7 Insert the needle back into the centre, bringing it out at the edge and work a hem stitch at each of the red marks (see P54).

8 To finish, remove the mushroom and bring the needle to the back of the work. Pass the needle through the stitches on the back.

9 The tambourine darn is complete.

Widening the tambourine stitch

1 Complete steps 1–6 on P42. Insert the needle inside the first loop and come out 1cm above.

2 Pass the thread behind the needle form right to left.

3 Insert the needle in the next loop bringing it out 0.5cm to the left. Pass the thread from right to left.

4 Skip the first stitch, or make two stitches. When the circle is complete, pick up the the first stitch as in step 6 on P42.

5 Remove the mushroom and bring the needle to the back. Thread the needle through the remaining stitches to finish.

6 The second round is complete. To widen the circle further, repeat steps 1 to 4.

Fan-shaped tambourine stitch

USES
Sweater

MATERIALS
Mixed fibre

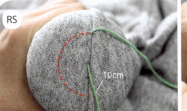   

1 Mark a semi-circle with chalk. Insert the needle into the centre of the straight line, bringing it out at one edge. Leave a 10cm tail.

2 Take the needle back to the centre and bring it out about 0.3–0.4cm to the left. Pass the thread from right to left behind the needle.

3 Repeat step 2, always going back to the centre, moving left around the marked curve.

4 Repeat step 3 until your fan is how you want it. Catch the last stitch as you pass the needle to the back.

5 Finish the thread at the back and trim the end (see P25).

6 The fan-shaped tambourine is complete. Enlarge the shape by following the steps for 'widening the tambourine stitch' above.

Brooches made with honeycomb and tambourine stitch

Finished size: 5 x 4.5cm

parallel honey-comb stitch (P38–39)

leave the ends unfinished

How to make

1 Stitch as shown.
2 Turn this into a millefeuille brooch (see P58).
3 Attach a brooch pin (P60–61).

MATERIALS
Three layers of rayon denim fabric (5 × 4.5cm)

I used some silver thread from my stash to make a parallel honeycomb stitch and this strange shape emerged.

No.
05 Sea bubble

Finished size 7.5cm diameter

dense honeycomb flower stitch (P40-41)

I cut up a traditional Oxford shirt and embroidered it with silk-wool thread to create this bubbly brooch

How to make

1 Stitch as shown.
2 Turn this into a macaron brooch (see P63–65).
3 Attach a brooch pin (P60–61).

MATERIALS
Front: cotton fabric cut from a shirt (16 × 16cm)
Filling: soft toy stuffing
Back: cotton sheeting (9 × 9cm)
Macaron mould: 7cm diameter

No.
06 Ruins

Finished size: 9cm x 13cm

How to make

1 Stitch as shown.
2 Turn this into a millefeuille brooch (see P58).
3 Attach a brooch pin (P60–61).

MATERIALS
Three layers of cloth: antique linen, wool felt and Indian cotton (all 9 × 13cm)

parallel honey-comb stitch from the back (P38–39)

tambourine stitch (P42–43cm)

A millefeuille brooch made from several layers of cloth. We called this one Ruins as it looks like the site of an archaeological dig.

No. 07 Blossom

Finished size: 5cm diameter

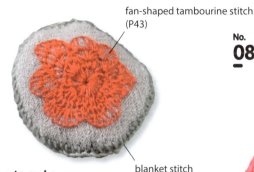

fan-shaped tambourine stitch
(P43)

blanket stitch
(P34–35)

How to make

1 Stitch as shown in the image above.
2 Turn this into a soft brooch (see p56–57).
3 Attach a brooch pin (p61).

You can create flowers using just the fan-shaped tambourine stitch. Make lots and they will vary depending on the cloth and thread you use.

MATERIALS
Front and back: two layers of woollen fabric (both 7 × 7cm)
Filling: soft toy stuffing

No. 08 Video games

Finished size: 6cm diameter

parallel honeycomb stitch (P38–39)

How to make

1 Stitch as shown.
2 Turn this into a macaron brooch (see P63–65).
3 Attach a kilt pin (P62).

This was inspired by the old video games we used to play. Neon colours fit the vibe. The background music was always the best bit.

MATERIALS
Front and lining: cotton jersey (fabric cut from a T-shirt 13 × 13cm and 8 × 8cm)
Button badge, 6cm diameter

loosely worked honeycomb stitch (P38–39)

parallel honeycomb stitch (P38–39)

allow the unfinished threads to hang loosely

No. 09 Waves

Finished size: 10 x 8.5cm

How to make

1 Stitch as shown in the photo.
2 Attach a kilt pin (see P61).

This was stitched with soft linen thread on a stretchy fabric. The ragged edge makes it unique. The thread is like a splash of water.

MATERIALS
Two layers of cotton jersey cut from a T-shirt (2 pieces 10 × 8cm)

Woven square darning

The English basket-stitch style is the most basic and traditional darning technique, where the warp threads are woven alternately. In this style, the fabric is caught by the needle while you are weaving the weft, meaning it blends in well.

1 Use a darning mushroom and chalk a square 0.5cm outside the damaged area. Cut a 50cm length of thread.

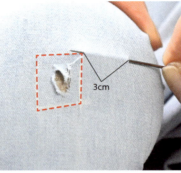

2 Thread the needle and insert 3cm away from the marked area. Bring out at the upper right corner of the mark.

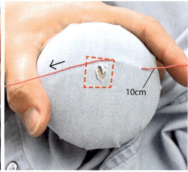

3 Pull the thread through, leaving a 10cm tail.

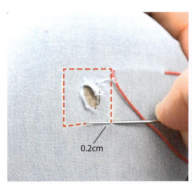

4 Insert the needle in the bottom right corner, bringing it out about 0.2cm to the left.

5 Pull the thread. One warp thread has been made.

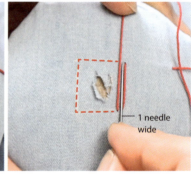

6 Pass the thread directly above and check the distance between the threads is about the width of your needle, .

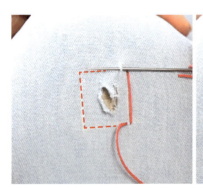

7 Make another stitch at the top of the square with the same one-needle's width spacing.

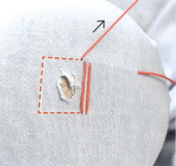

8 Pull the thread.

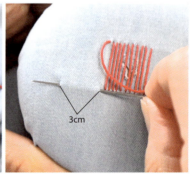

9 Repeat steps 7 and 8 until the square is filled, then bring the needle out about 3cm away.

USES
Shirt with holes made by my dungarees

MATERIALS
Sashiko or #8 embroidery thread

10 Pull the thread out and cut leaving a 10cm tail. All the warp threads have been worked.

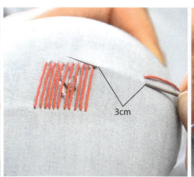

11 Start the weft. Using a new thread insert the needle 3cm away from the square, exiting at the upper right corner.

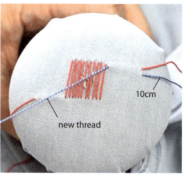

12 Pull the thread, leaving a 10cm tail.

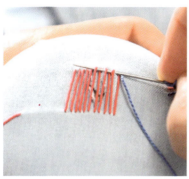

13 Pick up every alternate warp thread, the second, then the fourth etc. Pick a tiny bit of the base fabric where possible.

14 Pull the thread and continue as in step 13.

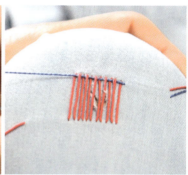

15 The first row is complete.

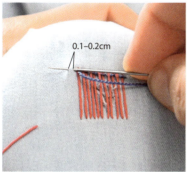

16 Make one small stitch (about 0.1–0.2cm) from right to left at the end of the row.

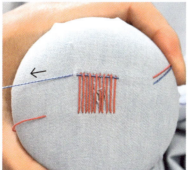

17 Pull the thread through. The first weft row is complete.

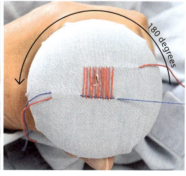

18 Turn the darning mushroom through 180 degrees.

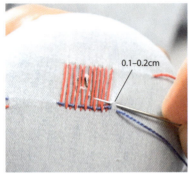

19 Make a small stitch at the right edge, picking up about 0.1–0.2cm of fabric.

20 Carry on threading the weft as steps 13 to 17 on P47. On the second row, work the opposite way to the first and repeat.

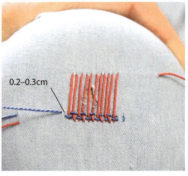

21 Make a small stitch at the end of the row.

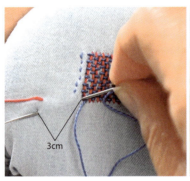

22 Repeat steps 18 to 21 until the square is covered. Take the needle out away from the marked area, leaving a tail.

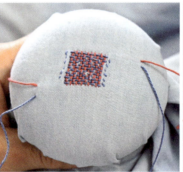

23 The weft is complete.

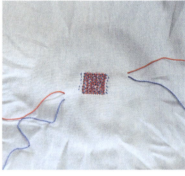

24 Remove the darning mushroom.

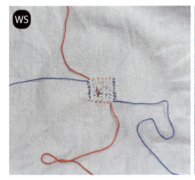

25 Pull the threads to the back of the work.

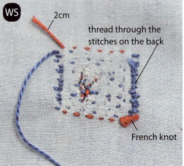

26 Finish the ends using your preferred method (see P25).

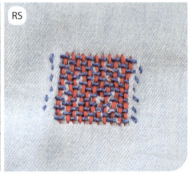

27 The woven square is complete. Applying steam from an iron will help the stitches to line up and settle into the fabric.

Brooches made with woven square darning

No. 10 Marie

Finished size: 8cm diameter
Tassel 7.5cm

woven darn
(P46–48)

tassel (P59)

How to make

1 Stitch as shown in the picture.
2 Finish into a soft brooch (P56–57).
3 Sew the tassel into the seam gap.
4 Attach a small kilt pin (P62).

MATERIALS
Front: cotton lawn (17 × 17cm)
Filling: soft toy stuffing
Lining: jersey (cut from a swimsuit 10 × 10cm)

This geometric pattern was created by making woven squares in a regular grid. The fluffy tassel makes it softer.

No. 11 Neon in the rain

Finished size: H 9.5cm W9cm

woven darn
(P46–48)

Denim has been made into an octagon with sharp corners. The bright colours stand out on the dark background.

How to make

1 Stitch as shown in the picture.
2 Finish into a soft brooch (P56–57).
3 Attach a brooch pin (P60–61).

MATERIALS
Front and back: denim fabric (19 × 19cm, 11 × 11cm)
Filling: soft toy stuffing

No. 12 Vintage tweed

Finished size: 7cm diameter

How to make

1 Stitch as shown in the picture.
2 Finish into a macaron brooch (P63–65).
3 Attach the brooch pin (P60–61).

woven darn (P46–48)

I chose the colour of the yarn to match the colour of the tweed fabric used for the base, and the result looks as if it has faded over time.

MATERIALS
Front: Tweed fabric (15 × 15cm)
Filling: soft toy stuffing
Lining: Corduroy (9 × 9cm)
Macaron mould 7cm diameter

Darning with appliqué

USES
Cotton-cashmere
sweater

MATERIALS
Button thread

When you have a large hole to mend or the fabric is torn, appliqué patches are useful. Use pretty prints and beautiful-coloured cloth and stitching with bright threads to add a colour accent while you are reinforcing. You can also choose similar colours to tone it down.

1 Cut a patch with scissors, or tear by hand. If you are concerned about the edges fraying, apply a layer of anti-fray glue.

2 Apply temporary adhesive to the area you want to repair.

3 Apply the patches and using tacking thread sew temporary stitches around the outline, to be a guide for the next step.

4 Turn over to the wrong side and mount the work on your darning mushroom.

5 Work a zigzag parallel honeycomb stitch (P38–39) inside the tacking marker for patch **A**.

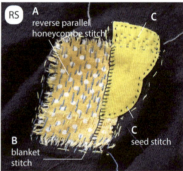

6 Remove the mushroom, turn over and reset. Apply blanket stitch (**B**, P34–35) and seed stitch (**C**, P30–31) as shown.

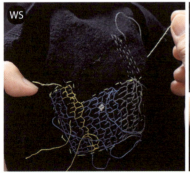

7 Pull the threads to the wrong side and remove the tacking stitches.

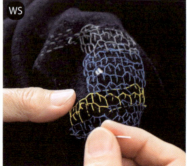

8 Finish the ends on the wrong side (see 25).

9 Your appliqué patch darn is complete.

Brooches made with appliqué

No. 13 Biscuit

Finished size: 12.5 x 15.5cm

appliqué
+
honeycomb stitch (P38–39)
+
seed stitch (P30–31)

honeycomb stitch (P38–39)

seed stitch (P30–31)

wool fabric
+
seed stitch (P30–31)

woven darn (P46–48)

How to make

1 Stitch as shown in the picture.
2 Finish into a soft brooch (P56–57).
3 Attach the kilt pin (P62).

MATERIALS
Front: wool fabric (17 × 17cm)
Filling: soft toy stuffing
Back: cotton broadcloth (14.5 x 17.5cm)

yarn, attached with running stitch (P28–29)

cotton flannel
+
seed stitch (P30–31)

cotton fabric (cut from an embroidered dress)
+
hem stitch (P54)

This pocket-shaped brooch is made from scraps of wool and a variety of stitches to create texture.

---

seed stitch (P30–31)

parallel honeycomb stitch (P38–39)

reverse honeycomb stitch (P36–37)

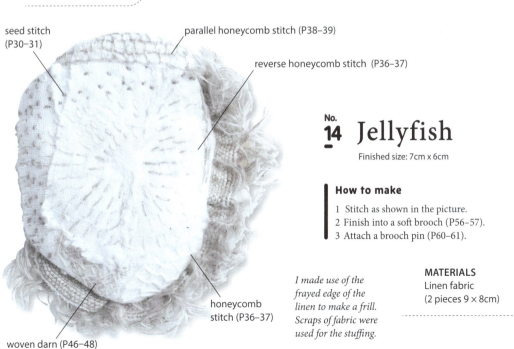

No. 14 Jellyfish

Finished size: 7cm x 6cm

How to make

1 Stitch as shown in the picture.
2 Finish into a soft brooch (P56–57).
3 Attach a brooch pin (P60–61).

MATERIALS
Linen fabric (2 pieces 9 × 8cm)

I made use of the frayed edge of the linen to make a frill. Scraps of fabric were used for the stuffing.

honeycomb stitch (P36–37)

woven darn (P46–48)

No. 15 Peacock

Finished size: H143cm W13cm

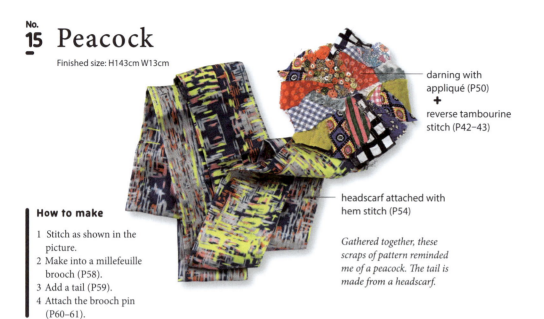

darning with appliqué (P50)
+
reverse tambourine stitch (P42–43)

headscarf attached with hem stitch (P54)

How to make

1 Stitch as shown in the picture.
2 Make into a millefeuille brooch (P58).
3 Add a tail (P59).
4 Attach the brooch pin (P60–61).

Gathered together, these scraps of pattern reminded me of a peacock. The tail is made from a headscarf.

MATERIALS

Front/back: printed cotton (2 pieces 13 x 13cm)
Filling: layers of cotton fabric

No. 16 Midsummer

Finished size: 12.5 x 13.5cm

How to make

1 Stitch as shown in the picture.
2 Make into a millefeuille brooch (P58).
3 Attach the kilt pin (P62).

MATERIALS

Front: cotton piqué, muslin, cotton voile (all 12.5 × 13.5cm)

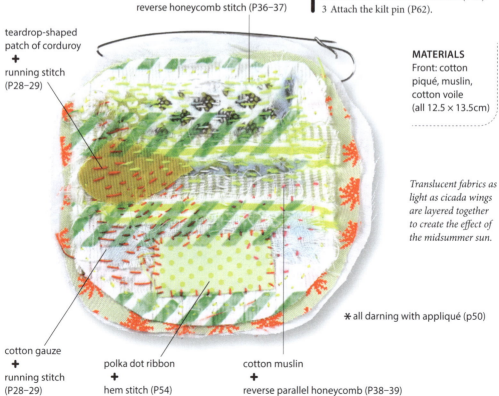

reverse honeycomb stitch (P36–37)

teardrop-shaped patch of corduroy
+
running stitch (P28–29)

Translucent fabrics as light as cicada wings are layered together to create the effect of the midsummer sun.

＊all darning with appliqué (p50)

cotton gauze
+
running stitch (P28–29)

polka dot ribbon
+
hem stitch (P54)

cotton muslin
+
reverse parallel honeycomb (P38–39)

No. 17 Between shadow and light

Finished size: H 9cm W 16cm

✷ all darning with appliqué (P50)

How to make

1 Stitch as shown.
2 Finish into a soft brooch (p56-57).
3 Attach the kilt pin (p62).

MATERIALS
Front: cotton lawn
(17 × 17cm)
Filling: cotton batting
Lining: plain weave cotton

cotton fabric
+
hem stitch (P54)

cotton fabric
+
reverse honeycomb stitch (P38–39)

cotton lawn
+
running stitch (P28–29)

striped hemp
+
seed stitch (P30–31)

rayon blend denim
+
reverse parallel honeycomb stitch (P38–39)

striped hemp cloth
+
running stitch (P28–29)

A collage of scraps that had been lingering in my sewing basket. The composition came by chance use of the shapes that I had.

No. 18 Precious

Finished size: H 10cm W 10cm

sequins (P54)

printed cotton
+
feather stitch (P54)

Denim
+
seed stitch (P30–31)

cotton lawn
+
Y-stitch (P54)

embroidered fabric
+
French knots (P54)

decorate the edges with chunky bouclé (P57)

bead stitch (P54)

wool knit
+
reverse parallel honeycomb stitch (P38–39)

cotton lawn
+
blanket stitch (P34–35)

linen fabric
+
lazy daisy stitch (P54)

corduroy
+
tambourine stitch (P42–43)

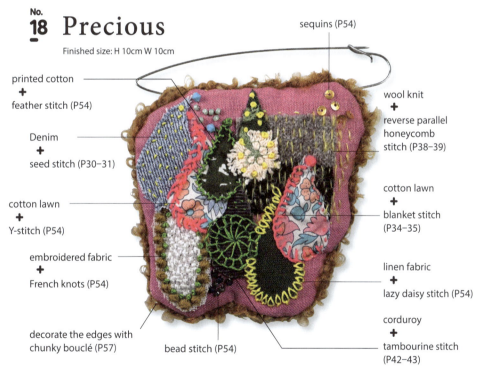

How to make

1 Stitch as shown in the picture.
2 Finish into a soft brooch (P56-57).
3 Attach the kilt pin (P62).

✷ all darning with appliqué (P50)

MATERIALS
Front: linen fabric (cut from an apron
12 × 12cm)
Filling: soft toy stuffing
Back: wool gauze (12 × 12cm)

The base of this brooch is a linen apron that has been used for many years. To match the bright pink, we finished it with colourful contrasting threads.

A variety of stitches

Using a darning mushroom means you won't have access to the back of the work, so you have to pick up the fabric from the front. Don't worry if the stitches aren't perfect! There are no rules, so find a stitching method that suits you.

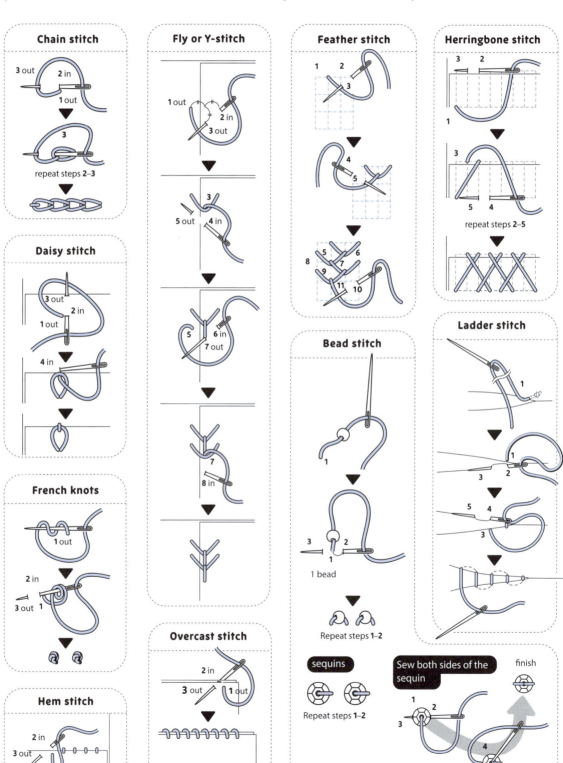

Chain stitch
3 out 2 in
1 out
3
repeat steps 2–3

Daisy stitch
3 out 2 in
1 out
4 in

French knots
1 out
2 in
3 out 1

Hem stitch
2 in
3 out
1 out

Fly or Y-stitch
1 out 2 in
3 out
3
5 out 4 in
5 6 in
7 out
7
8 in

Overcast stitch
2 in
3 out 1 out

Feather stitch
1 2
3
4
5
8 5 6
7
9
11 10

Bead stitch
1
3 2
1
1 bead
Repeat steps 1–2

sequins
Repeat steps 1–2

Herringbone stitch
3 2
1
3
5 4
repeat steps 2–5

Ladder stitch
1
1
3 2
5 4
3

Sew both sides of the sequin finish
1 2
3
4
3

54

Part 2

Making brooches

How to make a soft brooch

A soft brooch has an outer and a lining fabric, sewn together on the inside. You can use stuffing or scraps of cloth or threads to fill. Pack loosely – pack it too tightly and it may look like a soft toy.

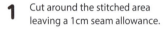

1 Cut around the stitched area leaving a 1cm seam allowance.

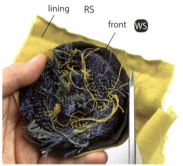

2 Cut the lining fabric to the same size.

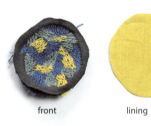

3 The outer material and the lining are cut to the same size and shape.

4 Place the front and back together, right sides facing each other. Sew around the seam with seed stitch leaving a 5–6cm opening.

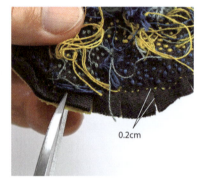

5 Make notches in the seam allowance, leaving a gap of 0.2cm from the seam, being careful not to cut the stitching.

6 Turn right side out through the opening.

7 Tear the filling into small amounts and insert bit by bit through the opening.

8 Tuck the seam allowance of the opening edges to the inside. Secure with pins and sew with ladder stitch (P54).

9 Make a knot at the edge to finish (P25).

USES
Cotton jersey
(cut from a T-shirt)
Corduroy (lining)

MATERIALS
Embroidery
thread

10 Insert the needle between the two pieces of fabric and bring out about 2 to 3cm away.

11 Pull the thread and trim the remaining ends.

12 Attach a brooch or kilt pin to complete the brooch (P60–62).

Decorating the edges

MATERIALS
Chunky bouclé mohair and other fluffy yarns

1 Thread the needle with fluffy yarn. Use the needle to find the row of stitches in the seam.

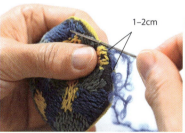

2 Pull the thread, leaving a tail of about 3cm. Use the needle to pick up stitches at 1–2cm intervals.

3 Pull the thread and repeat step 2.

4 Continue all the way around the edge twice.

5 After the second round cut off the excess thread.

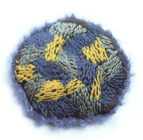

6 Adjust the shape and the brooch is complete.

How to make a millefeuille brooch

USES
Cotton
fabric, felt

MATERIALS
Sashiko
thread

This is a brooch made of many layers, like the tiers in a French pastry. We're using felt, but you can use any fabrics. Use this technique to make large works such as wall hangings, coasters and hot mats.

1 Cut around your darned cloth to create the desired shape.

felt

2 Layer the felt, a favourite fabric (in this case polka-dot) then the darned layer on the top. Secure with pins.

3 Sew around the edges using seed stitch, going through all three layers.

RS

4 Three layers sewn together.

WS

5 On the reverse you can see the stitches that outline the shape.

6 Trim the edges.

7 To make a fringe, cut notches at the edges of some of the fabric.

8 Rub the fringe with your hands to loosen it.

9 Attach a brooch, or kilt pin, if you like, to complete your brooch (P60–62).

Adding a fringe

Create a fringe by sewing ribbon or scraps of fabric on your brooch. Cut into the cloth and make the length and shape uneven, or make a fringe by unravelling threads or leaving the tails loose.

No. 19 June lane

Finished size: 5cm diameter

WS hem stitch (P54)

Fold a ribbon in half and sew along the fold at the back of your brooch. Try varying the length of the ends and make the fold diagonal.

No. 20 Colourful energy

Finished size: 16 x 14cm

blanket stitch (P34–35)

Layer fabrics or threads randomly and use a woven or honeycomb stitch. Attach a kilt pin with blanket stitch.

No. 21 Winter flower

Finished size: 10cm diameter

Use scraps of felt in the shapes as they come. Sew onto a felt base using seed stitch. Start from the centre and spread outwards.

seed stitch (P30–31)

Make a tassel

You can make a tassel from a hank of embroidery thread or floss. First, pull out about 50cm of the thread and divide it into three pieces, two of 15cm and one of 20cm.

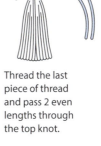

1 Using one of the shorter pieces of thread, tie a knot in the centre of the hank and remove the labels.

2 Fold the hank in half (the knot will be hidden). Wrap the longer thread around the top 3 times, with 1 end long and one short.

3 Thread the longer end and pass the needle back through the thread that's wound around. Trim the ends including the thread used to tie the top.

4 Thread the last piece of thread and pass 2 even lengths through the top knot.

5 Tie the two ends together, trim the ends and you're done.

Attach a brooch pin

This is an easy way to attach a sew-on brooch pin. The pin is attached to a swatch and sewn onto the brooch after it is finished. This technique makes it easier to adjust the position and there is less chance of the pin bending as you are sewing.

1 Cut a piece of cloth larger than the brooch pin and mark the position with chalk.

2 Thread a needle and tie a knot at the end. Insert the needle into the hole of the pin from the back.

3 Pull the thread.

4 Insert the needle around the edge of the pin.

5 Then come back up through the hole.

6 Repeat steps 4 and 5.

7 When you have sewn one side, turn the work 180 degrees and repeat steps 4 and 5 on the other side of the brooch pin.

8 Finish with a knot at the back (P25).

9 Next, insert the needle into the other hole in the brooch pin and pull the thread.

CLOTH USED	THREAD USED
Raw cotton	Button thread

10 Repeat steps 4 to 7.

11 Tie a knot at the back and cut off the excess thread.

12 The brooch pin is attached.

13 Position the swatch on the back of your motif and secure with pins. Thread a needle , knot the end and bring it out from back to front.

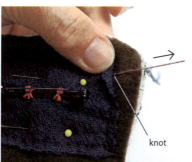

14 Pull the thread, then sew around the patch with seed stitch. At the end, turn over the edge of the cloth and make a knot to finish.

knot

seed stitch (P30–31)

15 Trim the excess thread on the back.

Bulb or coiless pins

Bulbous safety pins used for clothes tags or as stitch markers for knitting have no coils so don't get caught and can be attached anywhere. Use them to make a quick brooch or thread on a cord to make a necklace.

knit pin   bulb pin

Pin scraps

bulb pin

Fold your oddments loosely and attach a pin to complete a brooch.

Put on a necklace

knit pin

If you are attaching a brooch to beads or a chain, use two pins to stabilise it.

bulb pin

If you use a bulb pin, with no coil, you can hang the brooch like a pendant or charm.

How to attach kilt pins

Kilt pins are traditionally used to fasten stoles and the eponymous wraparound skirt. Make use of these pins to complement your creations. They can be sewn on or simply pinned, to suit your needs.

Fastening

back of brooch

kilt pin

RS

WS

RS

WS

If you are fastening the pin vertically, only pick up a small amount of fabric.

If you position the pin horizontally, scoop up more cloth.

Sewing on

kilt pin

blanket stitch (P34–35)

sew on kilt pin

fabric swatch

seed stitch (P30–31)

brooch motif

Sew the pin to a swatch of fabric using a blanket stitch, then place the base fabric on the back of the brooch motif and attach with seed stitch.

scraps of felt

kilt pin

seed stitch (P30–31)

Pieces of felt are layered on a kilt pin and sewn with a seed stitch.

Attach to bags or clothes

Position the brooch where you want to attach it, and scoop the bag and motif together with a kilt pin from the back.

How to make a macaron brooch

These are named after the sweetly-coloured Parisian meringues. A macaron mould can be from a fabric-covered button kit, bottle caps, tin badges, even walnut shells, or whatever is the right shape.

CLOTH USED
Fabric cut from a shirt
Lining cotton print

THREAD USED
Sashiko thread

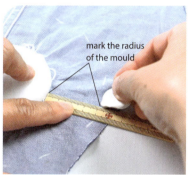

1 Place the macaron mould on the back of the darned cloth and mark a radius of the mould with chalk.

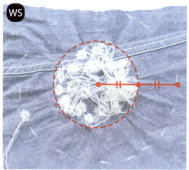

2 The centre of the brooch should be the centre of your shape.

3 Cut out the shape you have marked. Leaving the cotton threads inside will give your brooch a soft surface.

4 Cut out the lining to the same shape.

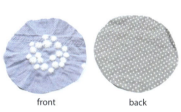

front   back

5 The outer material and lining are the same size.

6 Make the base for the back. Place the macaron mould on top of a clear plastic file and trace around it with a permanent marker.

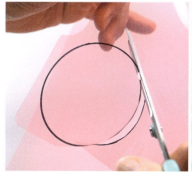

7 Cut out the shape with scissors.

8 Using sashiko thread, tie a knot, and sew with a large running stitch 1.5cm in from the edge of the outer fabric.

9 At the end of the round, pull the end to gather.

10 Tear the stuffing into small pieces, flatten it thinly, and spread it out to a size larger than the macaron mould.

11 Place the macaron mould on top, with the curved side facing down.

12 Pull the thread and gather together.

13 Turn over and adjust the pattern if it is out of place.

knot

14 When you are happy with the positioning, sew a knot on the back to secure.

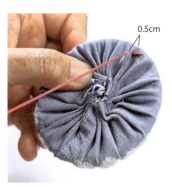

0.5cm

15 Using a double length of sashiko thread, tie a ball knot. Scoop one small stitch 0.5cm from the edge of the back.

0.5cm

16 Take a similar stitch 0.5cm from the opposite edge

17 Make another stitch back at the start.

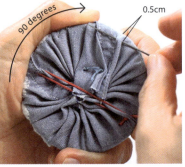

90 degrees

0.5cm

18 Rotate 90 degrees, scoop a small stitch 0.5cm from the edge, and pull the thread to tighten.

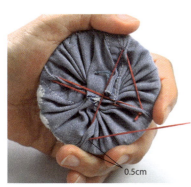

0.5cm

19 Pass the thread directly below, scoop a small stitch 0.5cm from the edge, and pull the thread to tighten.

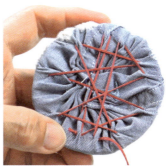

20 Repeat steps 18 and 19 while rotating the brooch, little by little.

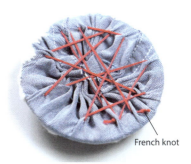

French knot

21 Finish with a knot and trim. This will tension the front and prevent the outer material from moving.

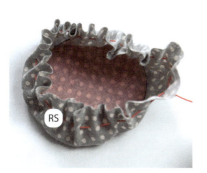

RS

22 To make the back, sew the lining with sashiko thread, as steps 8–9 on P63. Insert the circle, made in step 7, inside.

French knot

23 Gather the fabric and secure on the wrong side with a French knot to finish.

24 Place the back onto the under side of the front piece and pin in place.

25 Use hand sewing thread or button thread and work ladder stitch around the edges (P54).

26 Finish with a French knot, pull the knot inside, and cut off the excess thread.

27 Attach a brooch pin or kilt pin to the back to complete the macaron brooch (P60-62).

Macaron brooch variations

Macaron brooches can be darned using various materials and techniques. Whether finished with simple stitches or layered with colourful patchwork, you can pull it all together as a macaron brooch.

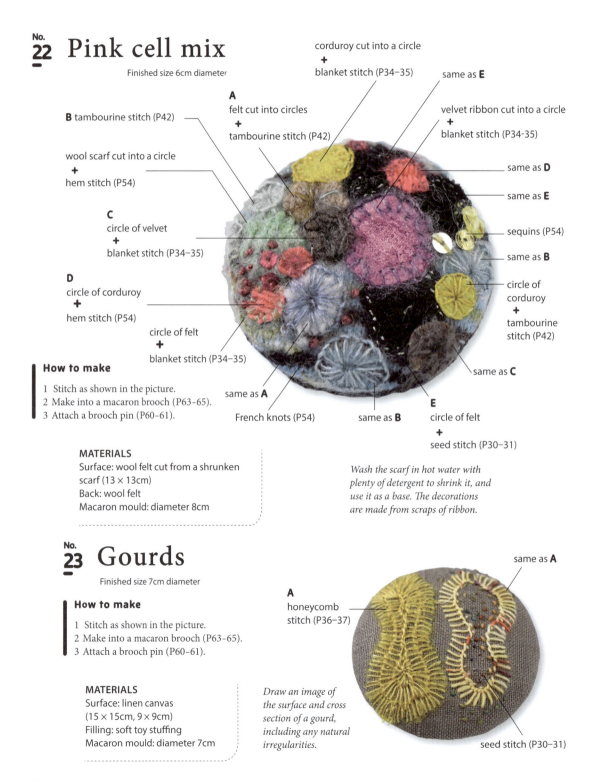

No. 22 Pink cell mix

Finished size 6cm diameter

corduroy cut into a circle
+
blanket stitch (P34–35)

same as **E**

A
felt cut into circles
+
tambourine stitch (P42)

velvet ribbon cut into a circle
+
blanket stitch (P34-35)

B tambourine stitch (P42)

same as **D**

wool scarf cut into a circle
+
hem stitch (P54)

same as **E**

sequins (P54)

C
circle of velvet
+
blanket stitch (P34–35)

same as **B**

circle of
corduroy
+
tambourine
stitch (P42)

D
circle of corduroy
+
hem stitch (P54)

circle of felt
+
blanket stitch (P34–35)

same as **C**

How to make

1 Stitch as shown in the picture.
2 Make into a macaron brooch (P63-65).
3 Attach a brooch pin (P60-61).

same as **A**

French knots (P54)

same as **B**

E
circle of felt
+
seed stitch (P30–31)

MATERIALS
Surface: wool felt cut from a shrunken scarf (13 × 13cm)
Back: wool felt
Macaron mould: diameter 8cm

Wash the scarf in hot water with plenty of detergent to shrink it, and use it as a base. The decorations are made from scraps of ribbon.

No. 23 Gourds

Finished size 7cm diameter

How to make

1 Stitch as shown in the picture.
2 Make into a macaron brooch (P63-65).
3 Attach a brooch pin (P60-61).

MATERIALS
Surface: linen canvas
(15 × 15cm, 9 × 9cm)
Filling: soft toy stuffing
Macaron mould: diameter 7cm

A
honeycomb
stitch (P36–37)

same as **A**

Draw an image of the surface and cross section of a gourd, including any natural irregularities.

seed stitch (P30–31)

No. 24 Summer constellation

Finished size 5cm in diameter

How to make

1 Stitch as shown in the picture.
2 Make into a macaron brooch (P63–65).
3 Attach a brooch pin (P60–61).

MATERIALS
Surface and back: Marimekko fabric (11 × 11cm, 7 × 7cm)
Filling: soft toy stuffing
Macaron mould: diameter 5cm

This uses my father's favourite tie, with a souvenir from his father who often travelled abroad. Now I can cherish it as a brooch,

A
tie fabric cut into a circle
+
blanket stitch (P34–35)

same as **A**

French knots (P54)

Marimekko fabric cut into circles
+
seed stitch (P30–31)

seed stitch (P30–31)

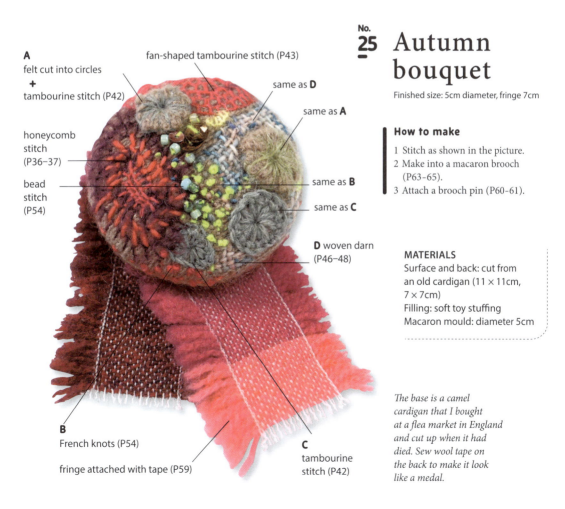

A
felt cut into circles
+
tambourine stitch (P42)

fan-shaped tambourine stitch (P43)

same as **D**

same as **A**

honeycomb stitch (P36–37)

bead stitch (P54)

same as **B**

same as **C**

D woven darn (P46–48)

B
French knots (P54)

fringe attached with tape (P59)

C
tambourine stitch (P42)

No. 25 Autumn bouquet

Finished size: 5cm diameter, fringe 7cm

How to make

1 Stitch as shown in the picture.
2 Make into a macaron brooch (P63–65).
3 Attach a brooch pin (P60–61).

MATERIALS
Surface and back: cut from an old cardigan (11 × 11cm, 7 × 7cm)
Filling: soft toy stuffing
Macaron mould: diameter 5cm

The base is a camel cardigan that I bought at a flea market in England and cut up when it had died. Sew wool tape on the back to make it look like a medal.

No. 26 Blue cells

Finished size: 7cm diameter

A teardrop denim shapes
+
reverse parallel honeycomb stitch (P34–35)

French knots (P54)

cotton fabric cut into circles
+
blanket stitch (P34–35)

B chunky bouclé mohair yarn
+
seed stitch (P30–31)

same as **C**

C tambourine stitch (P42)

felt cut into circles
+
tambourine stitch (P42)

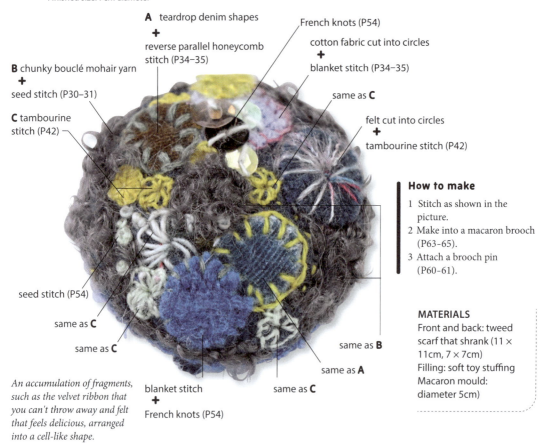

seed stitch (P54)

same as **C**

same as **C**

same as **B**

same as **A**

same as **C**

blanket stitch
+
French knots (P54)

An accumulation of fragments, such as the velvet ribbon that you can't throw away and felt that feels delicious, arranged into a cell-like shape.

How to make

1 Stitch as shown in the picture.
2 Make into a macaron brooch (P63–65).
3 Attach a brooch pin (P60–61).

MATERIALS
Front and back: tweed scarf that shrank (11 × 11cm, 7 × 7cm)
Filling: soft toy stuffing
Macaron mould: diameter 5cm)

No. 27 Galaxy hourglass

Finished size: 5cm diameter

How to make

1 Stitch as shown in the picture.
2 Make into a macaron brooch (P63–65).
3 Attach a brooch pin (P60–61).

MATERIALS
Front and back: wool flannel (11 × 11cm, 7 × 7cm)
Filling: soft toy stuffing
Macaron mould: diameter 5cm

reverse honeycomb stitch (P36–37)

honeycomb stitch (P36–37)

woven darn (P46–48)

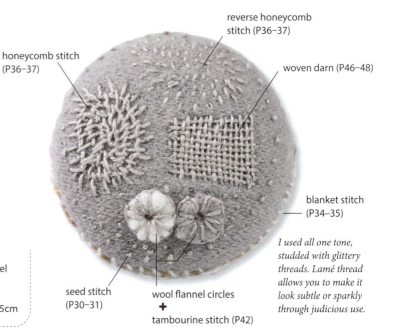

blanket stitch (P34–35)

I used all one tone, studded with glittery threads. Lamé thread allows you to make it look subtle or sparkly through judicious use.

seed stitch (P30–31)

wool flannel circles
+
tambourine stitch (P42)

No.
28 Denim petals

Finished size: 7cm diameter

How to make

1. Stitch as shown in the picture.
2. Make into a macaron brooch (P63–65).
3. Attach a brooch pin (P60–61).

MATERIALS

Front and back: denim dungaree fabric (15 × 15cm, 9 × 9cm)
Filling: soft toy stuffing
Macaron mould: diameter 7cm

Cut retro-prints from shirts and dresses into teardrop shapes. Stack them randomly to resemble petals floating on water.

A
teardrop denim shapes
+
reverse parallel honeycomb stitch (P38–39)

B
dress cut into a teardrop
+
reverse parallel honeycomb stitch (P38–39)

reverse parallel honeycomb (P38–39)

same as **A**

same as **B**

same as **A**

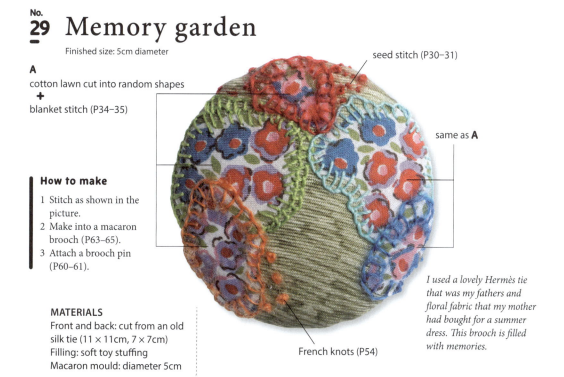

No.
29 Memory garden

Finished size: 5cm diameter

A
cotton lawn cut into random shapes
+
blanket stitch (P34–35)

How to make

1. Stitch as shown in the picture.
2. Make into a macaron brooch (P63–65).
3. Attach a brooch pin (P60–61).

MATERIALS

Front and back: cut from an old silk tie (11 × 11cm, 7 × 7cm)
Filling: soft toy stuffing
Macaron mould: diameter 5cm

seed stitch (P30–31)

same as **A**

French knots (P54)

I used a lovely Hermès tie that was my fathers and floral fabric that my mother had bought for a summer dress. This brooch is filled with memories.

Patch and brooch combinations

A darned patch can be made into a brooch or used to mend a garment. You can enjoy a variety of designs depending on how the patch is cut and arranged, as well as the type and method of stitching. Wonderful brooches can be made just by collaging random fabric scraps.

No. 30 Floating islands as seen by birds `circular patch`

Finished size: 16 x 20cm

before

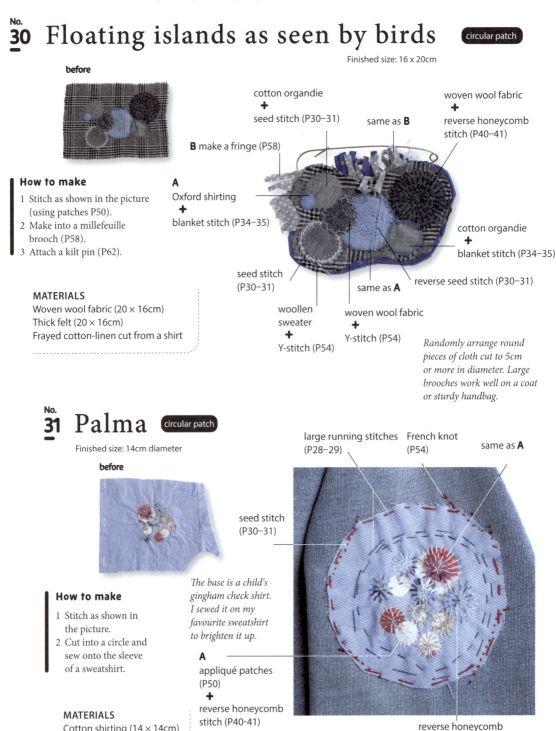

cotton organdie
+
seed stitch (P30–31)

same as **B**

woven wool fabric
+
reverse honeycomb stitch (P40–41)

B make a fringe (P58)

How to make

1 Stitch as shown in the picture (using patches P50).
2 Make into a millefeuille brooch (P58).
3 Attach a kilt pin (P62).

A
Oxford shirting
+
blanket stitch (P34–35)

cotton organdie
+
blanket stitch (P34–35)

reverse seed stitch (P30–31)

seed stitch (P30–31)

same as **A**

woollen sweater
+
Y-stitch (P54)

woven wool fabric
+
Y-stitch (P54)

MATERIALS
Woven wool fabric (20 × 16cm)
Thick felt (20 × 16cm)
Frayed cotton-linen cut from a shirt

Randomly arrange round pieces of cloth cut to 5cm or more in diameter. Large brooches work well on a coat or sturdy handbag.

No. 31 Palma `circular patch`

Finished size: 14cm diameter

before

large running stitches (P28–29)

French knot (P54)

same as **A**

seed stitch (P30–31)

How to make

1 Stitch as shown in the picture.
2 Cut into a circle and sew onto the sleeve of a sweatshirt.

The base is a child's gingham check shirt. I sewed it on my favourite sweatshirt to brighten it up.

A
appliqué patches (P50)
+
reverse honeycomb stitch (P40–41)

MATERIALS
Cotton shirting (14 × 14cm)

reverse honeycomb stitch (P40–41)

No.
32 Grimm `square patch` Square appliqué patches (P50)

Finished size: 7cm diameter

Floral print cotton and squares of cloth of various sizes and colours are sewn using sashiko, cashmere, and woollen threads.

before

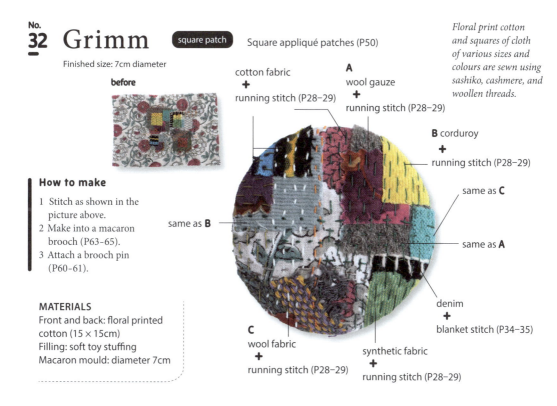

cotton fabric
+
running stitch (P28–29)

A
wool gauze
+
running stitch (P28–29)

B corduroy
+
running stitch (P28–29)

same as **C**

same as **A**

same as **B**

denim
+
blanket stitch (P34–35)

C
wool fabric
+
running stitch (P28–29)

synthetic fabric
+
running stitch (P28–29)

How to make

1 Stitch as shown in the picture above.
2 Make into a macaron brooch (P63-65).
3 Attach a brooch pin (P60-61).

MATERIALS
Front and back: floral printed cotton (15 × 15cm)
Filling: soft toy stuffing
Macaron mould: diameter 7cm

No.
33 Balancing trick `square patch`

Finished size: 17 x 22cm

before

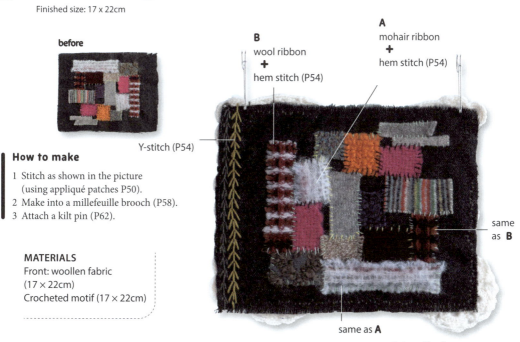

Y-stitch (P54)

B
wool ribbon
+
hem stitch (P54)

A
mohair ribbon
+
hem stitch (P54)

same as **B**

same as **A**

How to make

1 Stitch as shown in the picture (using appliqué patches P50).
2 Make into a millefeuille brooch (P58).
3 Attach a kilt pin (P62).

MATERIALS
Front: woollen fabric (17 × 22cm)
Crocheted motif (17 × 22cm)

Cut woollen fragments into rectangles and squares. The irregularity is part of it's charm.

34 Airy white cloud [square patch]

Finished size: 19 × 26cm

before

∗ darning with appliqué (P50)

organdie
+
seed stitch (P30–31)

cupro
+
running stitch (P28–29)

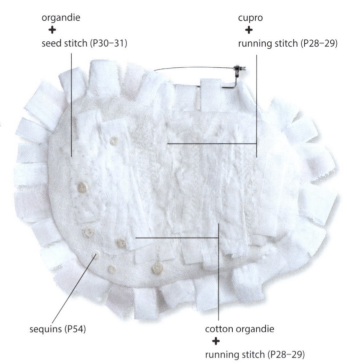

How to make

1 Stitch a patch as shown above.
2 Tear cloth into strips to make 2 x 7cm tapes (about 30) and fold each in half.
3 Pin to the edge of the outer material with the centre side facing out and match the lining to create a soft brooch (P56-57).

MATERIALS
Front: woven linen (fabric cut from pants 16 x 22 cm)
Filling: soft toy filling
Back: cotton organdie
(16 x 22cm)

sequins (P54)

cotton organdie
+
running stitch (P28–29)

Diaphanous white and pale fabrics create a large brooch that is light like a cloud or a heat haze. Hang by a window to let the light shine through.

No. 35 Highway [rectangular patch]

Finished size: 12 × 20cm

Liberty's peacock pattern a leopard print and corduroy are darned with seed stitch to create a grown-up brooch.

∗ darning with appliqué (P50)

running stitch
(P28–29)

same as **B**

before

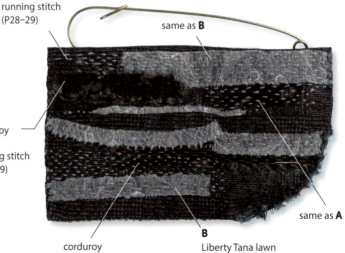

A
corduroy
+
running stitch
(P28–29)

How to make

1 Stitch as shown in the picture.
2 Finish into a soft brooch (P56–57).
3 Attach a kilt pin (P62).

MATERIALS
Front and back: wool tweed (16 × 24cm)
Synthetic fabric (16 × 24cm)

same as **A**

corduroy
+
seed stitch (P30–31)

B
Liberty Tana lawn
+
running stitch (P28–29)

No. 36 Story mountains

Finished size 17 × 23cm

before

A
linen shirt cut into triangles
+
reverse parallel honeycomb stitch (P38–39)

How to make

1 Stitch as shown in the photo.
2 Trim the excess jersey and sew on to the sweater.

MATERIALS
Cotton jersey from an old T-shirt (23 × 32cm)

I collected scraps of triangles that I made by chance and created the scenery of the mountain range. If you sew it roughly you can use it as a patch, then remove it and remake it into a brooch later.

✳ darning with appliqué (P50)

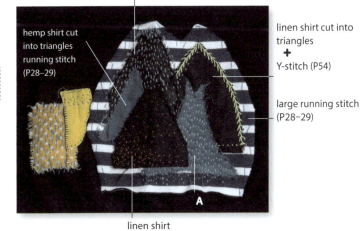

hemp shirt cut into triangles running stitch (P28–29)

linen shirt cut into triangles
+
Y-stitch (P54)

large running stitch (P28–29)

A

linen shirt
+
seed stitch (P30–31)

No. 37 Raindrops teardrop patch

Finished size: 23 × 22cm

before

How to make

1 Stitch as shown above.
2 Sew onto a tote bag.

MATERIALS
Jersey fabric cut from leggings (24 × 24cm)

This jersey fabric doesn't fray even if left unhemmed. I made a collage from the teardrop shapes and created a new pocket for this bag.

A tambourine stitch (P42)

C fan-shaped tambourine stitch (P43)

B honeycomb stitch (P36–37)   same as **C**

same as **A**

same as **B**

hem stitch (P54)

D seed stitch (P30–31)

same as **D**

same as **A**

same as **A**

reverse honeycomb stitch (P36–37)

hem stitch (P54)

same as **C**

chain stitch (P54)

same as **B**

appliqué patches in cotton jersey (P50)
+
reverse honeycomb stitch (P36–37)

same as **A**

✳ darning with appliqué (P50)

73

A collage of patches

1 Use any scraps that you have that are too small for anything else.

2 Play with the scraps until you have a composition that you like.

3 Apply the pieces as appliqué patches as on P50, then embellish over the top with stitching.

No. 38 Soaring ultramarine collage

Finished size: 13 x 14cm

Find a piece of denim that looks like it flutters and make it into a brooch with wings. The bright print in the centre is small but makes a real impact.

before

How to make

1 Stitch as show in the photo.
2 Finish as a soft brooch (P56–57).
3 Attach a brooch pin (P60–61).

MATERIALS
Front and back: woven wool fabric 13 × 14cm
Filling: soft toy stuffing

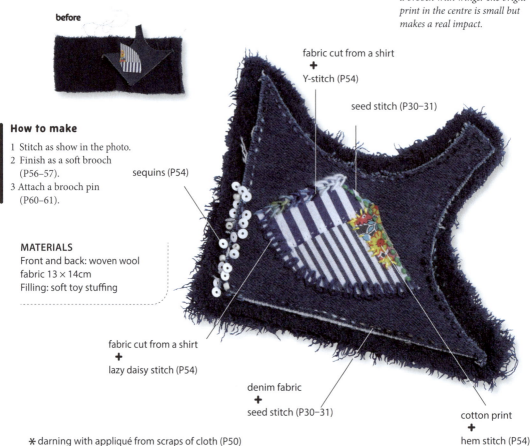

fabric cut from a shirt
+
Y-stitch (P54)

seed stitch (P30–31)

sequins (P54)

fabric cut from a shirt
+
lazy daisy stitch (P54)

denim fabric
+
seed stitch (P30–31)

cotton print
+
hem stitch (P54)

✽ darning with appliqué from scraps of cloth (P50)

Part 3

Enjoying your brooches

When layering macaron brooches, try slightly overlapping different sizes to create a good balance. By matching them with a patch brooch, you can counteract the sweetness of macaron brooches.

No. 39 Warm heart

Finished size: 6cm diameter

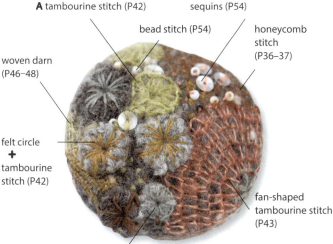

A tambourine stitch (P42)

sequins (P54)

bead stitch (P54)

honeycomb stitch (P36–37)

woven darn (P46–48)

felt circle
+
tambourine stitch (P42)

fan-shaped tambourine stitch (P43)

same as **A**

Gradually layer felt circles and circular stitching, then add sequins and beads to create your own style of brooch.

How to make

1. Stitch as shown in the photo.
2. Finish into a macaron brooch (P63–65).
3. Attach a brooch pin (P60–61).

MATERIALS
Front and back: tweed fabric from an old sweater (13 × 13cm, 8 × 8cm).
Filling: soft toy stuffing
Macaron mould: 6cm diameter

No. 40 Stone flower

Finished size: 5cm diameter

tambourine stitch (P42)

The embroidery on this desert rose radiates from the centre like petals on a flower.

How to make

1. Stitch as shown in the photo.
2. Finish into a macaron brooch (P63–65).
3. Attach a brooch pin (P60–61).

MATERIALS
Front and back: linen canvas (11 × 11cm, 6 × 6cm)
Filling: soft toy stuffing
Macaron mould: 5cm diameter

No. 41 Drystone wall

Finished size: 8 x 9.5cm

How to make

1. Stitch as shown in the image.
2. Attach a kilt pin (P61).

MATERIALS
wool fabric cut from a scarf (8 × 9.5cm)

This was inspired by the image of a wall I saw a long time ago, growing with plants and lichens. Change the look by placing the kilt pin vertically.

A
appliqué with wool (P50)
+
reverse parallel honeycomb stitch (P38–39)

appliqué wool ribbon (P50)
+
reverse parallel honeycomb stitch (P38–39)

tambourine stitch (P42)

same as **A**

No. 42 Weeds

Finished size: 5cm diameter

How to make

1 Stitch as shown in the photo.
2 Finish as a macaron brooch (P63-65).
3 Attach a brooch pin (P60-61).

MATERIALS

Front and back: wool tweed
(11 × 11cm, 7 × 7cm)
Macaron mould: 5cm diameter.

Triangular pieces of cloth were arranged in a radial pattern, then stitched from the outside towards the centre, changing the thickness of the thread on the way.

appliqué patches from twill fabric (P50)
+
reverse honeycomb stitch (P36–37)

No. 43 Oboro Kombu

Finished size: 7cm diameter

How to make

1 Stitch as shown in the photo.
2 Finish as a macaron brooch (P63-65).
3 Attach a brooch pin (P60-61).

MATERIALS

Front and back: wool gauze (15 × 15cm, 9 × 9cm)
Filling: soft toy stuffing
Macaron mould: 7cm diameter

A silk scarf was torn at the ends and was too weak for darning, so I ripped it and it turned into ribbon, that's like seaweed.

frills and torn strips (P32)

No. 44 Hashico

Finished size: 4 x 6cm

appliqué with strips of wool fabric (P50)
+
woven darn (P46–48)

overcasting (P54)

How to make

1 Stitch as shown in the photo.
2 Finish as a soft brooch (P56–57).
3 Attach a kilt pin (P62).

MATERIALS

Front and back: wool fabric (6 × 8cm)
Filling: soft toy stuffing

seed stitch (P30–31)

This is made with the leftovers from other projects. Even the threads are the collected ends. Use fine threads for a delicate feel.

A unique macaron brooch matches the model's hair band, with one looking almost like an earmuff. She also has a triangular brooch attached randomly to her hood.

This patchwork brooch is bold and decorative.
How to make the smaller square brooch is on P44.

This patch is sewn onto a jacket to make a new pocket, because you can never have too many pockets.

No.
45 Winter warmth

Finished size: 14 × 20cm

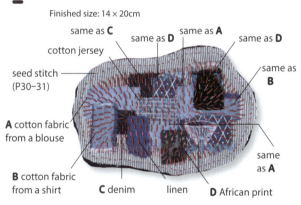

same as **C**
cotton jersey
same as **D**
same as **A**
same as **D**

seed stitch (P30–31)

same as **B**

A cotton fabric from a blouse

B cotton fabric from a shirt

C denim   linen   **D** African print

same as **A**

How to make

1　Sew as shown in the photo.
2　Make into a millefeuille brooch (P58).
3　Attach a brooch pin (P60-61).

✳ appliqué squares (P50)
✚
reverse honey-comb stitch (P36–37)

With cobblestones in mind, I layered scraps of squares and rectangles on top of each other. The red thread expresses warmth.

MATERIALS
Front: cotton (14 × 20cm)
Filling: synthetic felt (14 × 20cm)
Back: wool felt (14 × 20cm)

No.
46 Teardrops

Finished size: 21 × 17cm

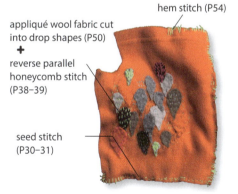

hem stitch (P54)

appliqué wool fabric cut into drop shapes (P50)
✚
reverse parallel honeycomb stitch (P38–39)

seed stitch (P30–31)

How to make

1　Sew as shown in the photo.
2　Attach it to a jacket.

The smallest scraps can be cut into teardrop shapes to make raindrops, abstract patterns or petals.

MATERIALS
Fabric cut from a fleece jacket (21 × 17cm)

81

Darning and patch brooches are placed randomly on a long shirt. Add a cushion brooch to your scarf for a totally unique look.

No. 47 Field

Finished size: 8 x 5cm

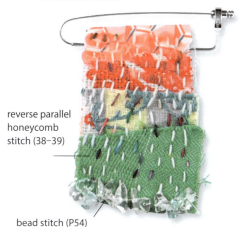

reverse parallel honeycomb stitch (38–39)

bead stitch (P54)

The scraps were layered and stitched rhythmically with space-dyed merino wool thread. The crystals are like bright lights.

How to make

1 Overlap 4 pieces of cloth, approx. 4 x 5cm.
2 Stitch as shown in the photo.
3 Sew crystal beads in a row on one end.
4 Attach a kilt pin (P62).

No. 48 Time machine

Finished size: 12cm diameter

seed stitch (P30–31)

add a fringe (P59)

How to make

1 Stitch as shown in the photo.
2 Finish as a soft brooch (P56–57).
3 Attach a kilt pin (P62).

Remember the summer holidays using fabrics your children used to wear. I added a dorsal fin to go with the beach theme.

MATERIALS
Front: cotton fabric cut from some children's shorts (14 × 14cm)
Filling: soft toy stuffing
Back: denim (14 x 14cm)

No. 49 Sea life

Finished size: 8 × 10cm

How to make

1 Sew as shown in the photo.
2 Make into a millefeuille brooch (P58).
3 Attach a kilt pin (P62).

MATERIALS
Cotton striped fabric (8 × 10cm)
Wool felt (8 × 10cm)

This rayon embroidery thread has a lovely sheen. Honeycomb stitch looks great on this stripy fabric too.

A parallel honeycomb stitch (P38–39)

French knots (P54)

same as **A**

same as **A**

No. 50 Yamabiko

Finished size:
- **a** 13cm × 10cm
- **b** 11 × 6cm **c** 8 × 11cm

✳ appliqué with triangles (P50)

✚ seed stitch (P30–31)

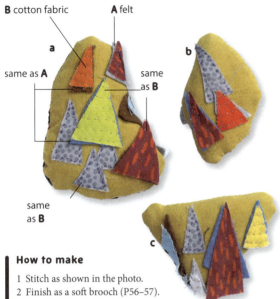

B cotton fabric **A** felt

same as **A**

same as **B**

same as **B**

How to make
1 Stitch as shown in the photo.
2 Finish as a soft brooch (P56–57).
3 Attach a kilt pin (P62).

MATERIALS
Front and back: corduroy (15 × 21cm)
Filling: soft toy stuffing

In Japanese folklore the Yamabiko is a mountain spirit, said to be responsible for echoes and mysterious noises that can be heard in the mountains.

No. 51 Me, me, me

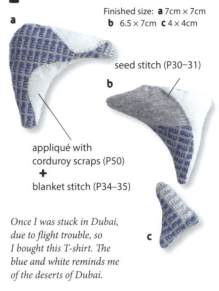

Finished size: **a** 7cm × 7cm
b 6.5 × 7cm **c** 4 × 4cm

seed stitch (P30–31)

appliqué with corduroy scraps (P50)

✚ blanket stitch (P34–35)

Once I was stuck in Dubai, due to flight trouble, so I bought this T-shirt. The blue and white reminds me of the deserts of Dubai.

How to make
1 Stitch as shown in the photo.
2 Finish as a soft brooch (P56–57).
3 Attach a safety pin (P61).

MATERIALS
Front and back: cotton jersey cut from a T-shirt 10 × 14cm
Filling: soft toy stuffing

No. 52 Moonlit walk

Finished size: 9 × 8cm

How to make
1 Stitch as shown in the photo.
2 Finish as a soft brooch (P56–57).
3 Attach a kilt pin (P62).

MATERIALS
Front and back: knitted wool (9 × 8cm cut from an old scarf)
Filling: old T-shirt fabric

appliqué with wool fabric (P50)
✚ reverse honeycomb stitch (P36–37)

honeycomb stitch (P36–37)

This depicts a person strolling on a moonlit night. The folded T-shirt stuffing inside gives it a firm body.

appliqué with wool fabric (P50)
✚ blanket stitch (P34–35)

French knots (P54)

honeycomb stitch with chunky bouclé thread (P36–37)

seed stitch (P30–31)

chain stitch (P54)

appliqué with cotton fabric (P50)
✚ reverse honeycomb stitch (P36–37)

mohair fringe with hem stitch (p54)

knitted wool fabric

Add a brooch to the strap of your bag to create an interesting back view.
Using kilt pins allows several brooches to hang freely like charms.

Attach a soft brooch to a long necklace for impact. Part of the charm of soft brooches is that they are large, but light, so they stay put. Instructions on P61.

Make a soft brooch into a bag charm with a giant kilt pin. The addition of a dark pink macaron brooch sobers up the kitsch bird.

No. 53   Poisson d'avril

Finished size: 8.5 × 15cm

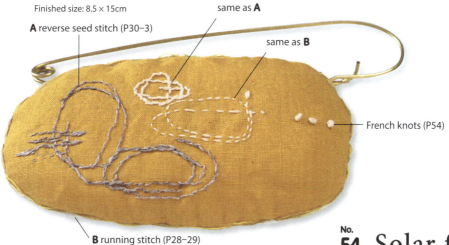

A reverse seed stitch (P30–3)

same as **A**

same as **B**

French knots (P54)

B running stitch (P28–29)

How to make

1 Stitch as shown in the photo.
2 Finish as a soft brooch (P56–57).
3 Attach a kilt pin (P62).

I stitched my favorite linen fabric with cashmere thread, tracing the trajectory of a doodle.

MATERIALS
Front: linen fabric
(10.5 × 17cm)
Filling: soft toy stuffing
lining: silk fabric (10.5 × 17cm)

No. 54   Solar flare

Finished size: 6cm diameter

honeycomb stitch (P38–39)

All the dark reds make this brooch like a blazing solar flare or a spicy curry on a hot day.

How to make

1 Stitch as shown in the photo.
2 Finish as a macaron brooch (P63–65).
3 Attach a kilt pin (P62).

MATERIALS
Front and back: linen
(13 × 13cm, 8 × 8cm)
Filling: soft toy stuffing
Macaron mould: 6cm

No. 55   Kitsch bird

Finished size 10 × 7cm

tambourine stitch (P42)

parallel honeycomb stitch (P38–39)

bead stitch (P54)

How to make

1 Stitch as shown in the photo.
2 Finish as a soft brooch (P56–57).
3 Attach a brooch pin (P60–61).

French knots (P54)

Decorate the edges with chunky bouclé mohair yarn (P57)

This bird started life on a cushion cover that I loved as a child. Neon coloured thread and glittery yarn make it sugary sweet.

MATERIALS
Front and back: Fabric cut from the cushion cover (12 × 9cm)
Filling: soft toy stuffing

No. 56 Buds

Finished size: 6cm diameter

bead stitch (P54)

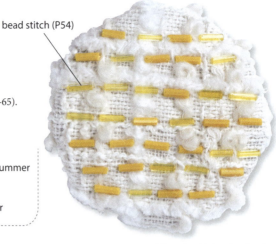

How to make

1 Stitch as shown in the photo.
2 Finish as a macaron brooch (P63–65).
3 Attach a brooch pin (P60–61).

MATERIALS
Front and back: cotton-linen summer tweed (13 × 13cm, 8 × 8cm)
Filling: soft toy stuffing
Macaron mould: 6cm diameter

A brooch with bamboo beads sewn onto summer tweed fabric. You can also wear it as a pendant by attaching to a chain of loosely crocheted yarn

No. 57 Sports day sun

Finished size: 7.5cm diameter

same as **A**

A blanket stitch (P34–35)

I cut up my old gym kit from primary school and used space-dyed thread to imagine a sunny school sports day.

circle of cotton jersey (from an old gym kit) appliqué patching (P50)
+
blanket stitch (P34–35)

circle (cut from a red and white hat) appliqué darning (P50)
+
seed stitch (P30–31)

How to make

1 Stitch as shown in the photo.
2 Finish as a soft brooch (P56–57).
3 Attach a brooch pin (P60–61).

MATERIALS
Front: cotton from old hat (8 × 8cm)
Filling: soft toy stuffing
Back: polyester jersey from old gym kit (9 × 9cm)

fan-shaped tambourine stitch (P43)

No. 58 Romanesco

Finished size: 9 × 9cm, fringe 22cm

How to make

1 Stitch as shown in the photo.
2 Finish as a soft brooch (P56–57).
3 Attach a brooch pin (P60–61).

MATERIALS
Front: cotton gingham (11 × 11cm)
Filling: soft toy stuffing
Back: velvet (11 × 11cm)

attach a fringe with torn linen (P59)

Spread the fan-shaped tambourine stitch radially, to look like a Romanesco cauliflower. Soften the look by adding a fringe to the wonky shape.

Instantly transform your brooches into a pendant or bag charm with loosely crocheted yarn to make a chain, or use the fringe to attach it.

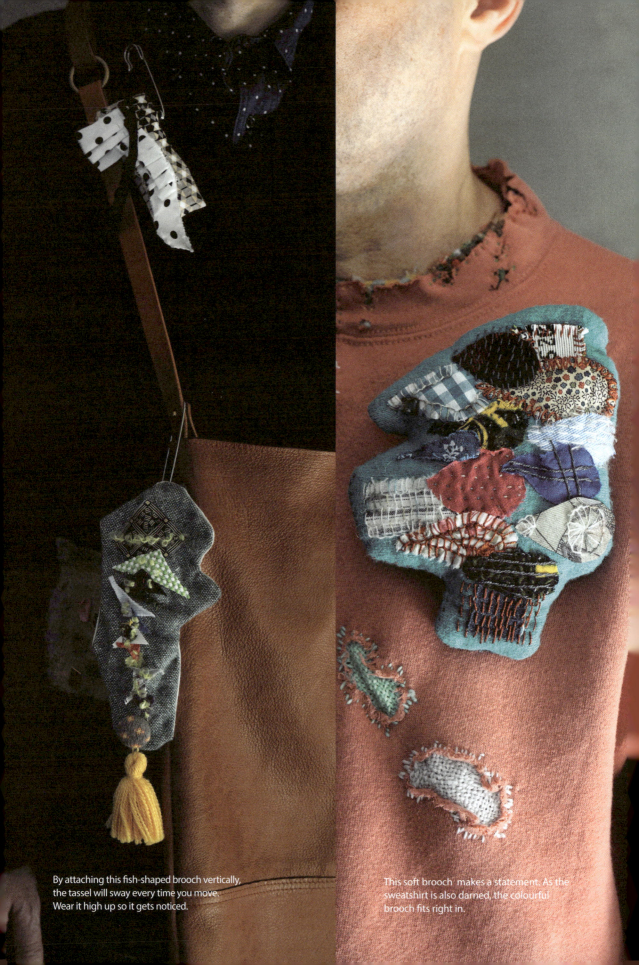

By attaching this fish-shaped brooch vertically, the tassel will sway every time you move. Wear it high up so it gets noticed.

This soft brooch makes a statement. As the sweatshirt is also darned, the colourful brooch fits right in.

Cotton fabric with a glossy geometric pattern is made into a plump soft brooch. The polka dot ruffles look like piano keys.

seed stitch (P30–31)

French knots (P54)

A delicate frills with cotton fabric (P32)

same as **A**

No. 59 Dance

Finished size: 11 × 4cm

How to make

1 Stitch as shown in the photo.
2 Finish as a soft brooch (P56–57).
3 Attach a kilt pin (P62).

MATERIALS
Cotton fabric cut from a skirt (13 × 6cm)
Filling: soft toy stuffing

No. 60 Ancient Fish

Finshed size: 10 × 21cm

How to make

1 Stitch as shown in the photo.
2 Finish as a soft brooch (P56–57).
3 Insert the string of the tassel into the seam and sew to secure.
4 Attach a kilt pin (P62).

MATERIALS
Front: wool tweed (12 × 23cm)
Filling: soft toy stuffing
cotton-linen fabric (12 × 23cm)

all appliqué (P50)
+
seed stitch (P30–31)

velvet

linen

wool felt

button

silk fabric

Triangular scraps were pieced together to create a fish shape, accented with a tassel made from lambswool yarn.

jersey

A cotton fabric

same as **A**

cashmere knit

tassel (P59)

cotton lawn
+
lazy daisy stitch (P54)

woven fabric
+
parallel honeycomb stitch (P38–39)

cotton fabric
+
reverse parallel honeycomb stitch (P38–39)

linen fabric
+
reverse seed stitch (P30–31)

wool fabric
+
reverse parallel honeycomb stitch (P38–39)

cotton gingham
+
honeycomb stitch (P36–37)

A turquoise sweater was cut and darned with colorful fabric. The inspiration was a dark forest where not much light enters.

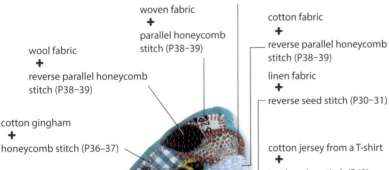

cotton jersey from a T-shirt
+
tambourine stitch (P42)

African print
+
reverse seed stitch (P30–31)

denim squares
+
reverse parallel honey-comb stitch (P38–39)

No. 61 Forest

Finshed size: 18 × 15cm

How to make

1 Stitch as shown in the photo.
2 Finish as a soft brooch (P56–57).
3 Attach a kilt pin (P62).

MATERIALS
Front: wool fabric (20 × 17cm)
Filling: soft toy stuffing
Back: cotton fabric (20 × 17cm)

African print
+
seed stitch (P30–31)

linen
+
seed stitch (P30–31)

linen cut into rectangles
+
parallel honeycomb stitch (P38–39)

seed stitch (P30–31)

cotton print
+
honeycomb stitch (P36)

✳ all appliqué (P50) cut everything into teardrop shapes

No. 62 Floating pollen

Finished size: 6.5 × 6cm

fan-shaped tambourine stitch (P43)

same as **A**

A tambourine stitch (P42)

I selected colourful, space-dyed thread that matched the frosty grey and tambourine stitch to create a cloud of pollen.

How to make

1 Stitch as shown in the photo.
2 Finish as a soft brooch (P56–57).
3 Attach a safety pin (P61).

MATERIALS
Front and back: cotton jersey (torn from a T-shirt, 8.5 × 8cm)
Filling: soft toy stuffing

No. 63 Cell division

Finished size: **a** 7 x 2.5cm **b** 8 × 5cm

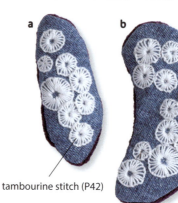

a

b

tambourine stitch (P42)

How to make

1 Stitch as shown in the photo.
2 Finish as a soft brooch (P56–57).
3 Attach a safety pin (P61).

MATERIALS
Front: denim (fabric cut from trousers, 13 × 13cm)
Filling: soft toy stuffing
Back: knit fabric (from a sweater, 13 × 13cm)

No. 62 Sea and sky

Finished size: 17 x 30cm

How to make

1 Stitch as shown in the photo.
2 Attach to the front of a shirt with long stitches.

MATERIALS
Front: shirting (17 × 30cm)

Darning with leftover cloth from shirts. I made a collage with some of the mysterious shapes that were made by chance.

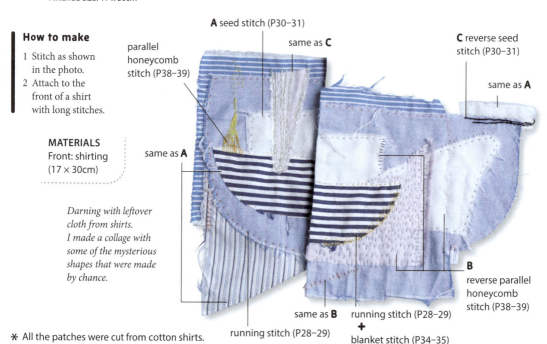

A seed stitch (P30–31)

same as **C**

C reverse seed stitch (P30–31)

same as **A**

parallel honeycomb stitch (P38–39)

same as **A**

B reverse parallel honeycomb stitch (P38–39)

same as **B**

running stitch (P28–29)
+
blanket stitch (P34–35)

running stitch (P28–29)

✱ All the patches were cut from cotton shirts.

This combination of red beads and a patched shirt works really well. If you are hanging brooches on a necklace, odd numbers are more balanced than even.

Conclusion

To date, I have taught darning techniques to many people both in Japan and abroad and I have shared my love for the things around us with many people. One of the things I hear often is comments such as, "I like the technique and spirit of darning, but it's difficult to wear clothes that have actually been darned."

Making darned macaron brooches is one of the modules in my darning classes. It is very popular because it allows you to quickly recreate the main darning techniques in a circle with a diameter of about 6cm, it can be finished in your favourite colour and is easy to wear.

Sometimes it's difficult to apply darning directly to the damaged area of a garment, so if you use a patch that is darned on a separate fabric, you can make it again if you don't like it, and you can change the position, size, number and design of the brooch later. Freestyle mending is born!

As I prototyped, improved, and taught darning macaron brooches, I was able to expand beyond the framework of macarons and develop them into soft brooches, mascots, charms – and even cushions if I enlarged them – and they have evolved.

Cloth cut from old clothes feels nicer to the touch, makes you feel happy just by touching it and is easy to wash when it gets dirty. I hope that the darning brooch gently promotes these sensitivities.

Needlework is a pleasure in its own right, and in the time spent stitching, one gets a sense of the history of these old fabrics, the colour, feel – stains and damage too in the case of old clothes. It makes me nostalgic, and gets me to thinking about my loved ones and wanting to make something for them.

I cherish the things that are important to me and the things I have a connection with by preserving them in the form of a brooch. I would be so happy if you could enjoy this process too.

Lastly, I would like to thank Ayako Kohyama, Madoka Saito, and Kaori Nakasuka of the HIKARU NOGUCHI Japan Darning Association for prototyping, researching and developing the darning brooches in the production of this book.

Work was also made by Kumiko Inoko, Michiko Urano, Junko Okuda, Mayumi Okuda, Nami Ogushi, Kumiko Shimizu, Yukie Tejima, Mami Nakamura, Maki Tobise, Hitomi Fukushima and Yoshihito Fukushima. We would like to express our thanks to the editorial and production teams who worked on the book.

Place fragments of fabric filled with precious memories one by one, until you like the design. I made this collage into a number of brooches.

tie lining

Mother's summer dresses

a Scandinavian souvenir

corduroy

Father's Hermès tie

Kitsch bird P87

Patch collage P74

Summer constellation P67

Hikaru Noguchi

Textile designer of her eponymous knitwear brand Hikaru Noguchi, and Japan Darning Association, Hikaru graduated from Musashino Art University, Tokyo, then studied textile design in the United Kingdom. Based in Japan, the United Kingdom, and South Africa, she has presented collections of knitwear designs in the fashion and interiors. Her activities include textile-related design, consulting, and writing around the world. In recent years, she has sparked the popularity of darning, teaching a large number of people in classes and workshops both domestically and internationally. Researching original darning techniques on a daily basis, she also produces original darning tools and stitching threads.

Online shop for original products
https://hikarunoguchi.shop
Instagram @hikaru_noguchi_design
@darning_by_hikaru_noguchi

Japanese team

Photos | Wakana Baba

Step photos | Miho Urushido

Step photo assistant |
Ayana Inukai

Design | Moe Hirota Bunkyo
Design Room

Illustrations | Masami Nagai

Models | Mimi Mashiko, Mami
Mashiko, Dominic Dawson

UK team

Editor | Katy Bevan

Typesetting | Chris J Bailey

Printed in the UK by Cambrian

Credits
Hikaru Noguchi
P33 No.02, P44 No.04, P44 No.05, P45 No.07, P49 No.12, P52 No.16, P53 No.17, P66 No.22, P67 No.24 No.25, P68 No.26, P69 No.28 No.29, P70 No.30, P72 No.34, P73 No.36, P74 No.38, P77 No.39, P81 No.46, P84 No.51, P87 No.55, P92 No.62 No.63 No.64

Kaori Nakasuka
P33 No.03, P44 No.06, P49 No.10, P51 No.13, P53 No.18, P66 No.23, P77 No.40, P81 No.45, P87 No.54, P88 No.58, P91 No.60 No.61

Ayako Kohyama
P70 No.31, 71 No.32, P72 No.35, P73 No.37, P83 No.48, P84 No.52, P87 No.53, P91 No.59

Madoka Saito
P33 No.01, P45 No.08 No.09, P49 No.11, P52 No.15, P59 No.19, P71 No.33, 77 No.41, P78 No.43, P83 No.49, P84 No.50

Kumiko Inoko
P59 No.21, P78 No.42, P83 No.47, P88 No.56

Kumiko Shimizu P51 No.14

Junko Okuda P59 No.20

Nami Ogushi P68 No.27

Mami Nakamura P78 No.44

Yoshihito Fukushima P88 No.57
with assistance from **Mayumi Okuda** and **Yukie Tejima**

Thanks for materials

Wallace Sewell Instagram @wallacesewell

Maiko Dawson Instagram @maikodawson

UK supplies from your local yarn store and

www.loopknitting.com @looplondonloves

www.raystitch.co.uk @raystitch

www.macculloch-wallis.co.uk @maccullochw

Beyond Darning

© 2024 Hikaru Noguchi

Hikaru Noguchi is hereby identified as the author of this work in accordance with section 77 of the Copyright, Designs and Patent Act, 1988. She asserts and gives notice of her moral right under this Act.

Published by Quickthorn
info@quickthornbooks.com
www.quickthornbooks.com
@quickthornbooks

Originally published in Japanese as *Darning Brooches* by Yama Kei, 2023

MIX
Supporting responsible forestry
FSC® C013417

Printed in the UK on FSC certified paper

British Library Cataloguing in Publication Data applied for
ISBN 978-1-7393160-44